It's Like Riding a
Bike

How to Make Learning Last a Lifetime

David M. Schmittou, Ed.D.

ARCHWAY
PUBLISHING

Archway Publishing books may be ordered through booksellers or by contacting:

Archway Publishing
1663 Liberty Drive
Bloomington, IN 47403
www.archwaypublishing.com
1 (888) 242-5904

Because of the dynamic nature of the Internet, any web addresses or links contained in this book may have changed since publication and may no longer be valid. The views expressed in this work are solely those of the author and do not necessarily reflect the views of the publisher, and the publisher hereby disclaims any responsibility for them.

Any people depicted in stock imagery provided by Thinkstock are models, and such images are being used for illustrative purposes only. Certain stock imagery © Thinkstock.

ISBN: 978-1-4808-4512-1 (sc)
ISBN: 978-1-4808-4513-8 (e)

Library of Congress Control Number: 2017904279

Print information available on the last page.

Archway Publishing rev. date: 3/21/2017

Contents

Introduction

Let's Think about It Differently

America. The greatest country on earth. We have people from around the world risking their lives to come here and access the dreams and opportunities this land offers. We tell our children from the time they start school that they can do and become anything they want if they simply work hard.

I have traveled the globe, and there is nowhere I would rather be than here. As an educator of America's youth, one of my charges is to keep it that way. I need to prepare our young people to keep our country thriving, to keep innovation alive, and to keep our businesses prospering. I feel this preparation is becoming increasingly difficult. This isn't because we aren't doing things right; it's because we aren't doing all we can while others around the world—those with seemingly nothing to lose by trying to do things differently—are quickly catching up and in many instances passing us by.

We have all seen the PISA (Program for International Student Assessment) reports that show American students lagging behind their counterparts in Asia and Europe in reading and math. We have high school dropout rates hovering around 50 percent for multiple subgroups of students, most notably African-American males. All the while, legislators are altering state standards, enacting more-restrictive testing, and mandating student retention.

Since the enactment of No Child Left Behind more than a decade ago and the more recent Every Child Succeeds Act, one would think we would begin to see student achievement rise, yet what we are seeing is the opposite. Student SAT scores are dipping in all subjects, college and career readiness are at all-time lows, and many legislators are running around throwing their arms in the air wondering what's going wrong. Some are arguing, quite persuasively I might add, that we need to put an even bigger emphasis on reading. It has been said that the more a student reads, the more he or she will learn. That statement and the mind-set that goes along with it have been trumpeted so often and so loudly that they are often stated and believed without a second thought.

But what if that isn't true? What if that simple statement, which drives virtually every initiative of public education across America, is actually leading us astray? Almost every state and federal mandate enacted to curb student achievement deficits is built on this premise, yet we are still not seeing the success we all hope for. It is possible that we are missing the mark when it comes to implementing the mandates. Just maybe, we have it all wrong.

Far too often, we have made school so completely isolated from the real world that as educators we have lost sight of what our primary mission is. If we want kids to learn to swim, we put them in the water. If we want students to be prepared for the world, we need to put them in the world. We have to get beyond crafting buildings and classrooms that are so far removed from any real-life settings that our students gain no real knowledge of how to apply learning and thinking strategies in their future.

To move our students into an environment of supportive risk taking, we as lead learners must do likewise. It's not enough for us to simply encourage our students to take risks; we must be willing to do so ourselves and find others who will lift us up when we fall. Teachers must embrace our students' drives, desires, and abilities to take chances in a safe and secure environment. We must motivate and celebrate. We must set goals and allow for learning to occur even through temporary failure.

We teachers must be willing to have conversations with our peers, but this is terrifying for so many of us. Actually speaking our minds and challenging the status quo can be difficult. Still others of us may look at this and think, *That's a piece of cake. I have no problem talking to my peers. I always get what I want.* That may be exactly why so many others are afraid of it.

Some people enter conversations with predetermined wills to get their ways, and others walk into conversations with no desire to debate. This is not about certain people imposing their wills on others; it's about fostering a rich, honest conversation about our children's destinies.

Teachers must be prepared to debate their feelings and share their biases to explain why they believe standards, engagement, assessments—any instructional practices they implement in their classrooms—are important. There will be debate, compromise, changed minds, and conflict. Change is difficult especially in schools run by people who were so good at playing school when they were kids. But today's kids are different, and so are their needs. As teachers, leaders, change agents, and destiny shapers, we must embrace our power to decide what and how our students will learn from us. Sometimes, using a well-crafted metaphor is all that we need to get the dialogue started. Throughout history, great teachers have used metaphors, parables, and stories to present their points. There is a reason all the great religions use narratives to detail what constitutes virtuous living. Metaphors allow us to reflect on our own practices and beliefs without a direct affront to who we are and what we do. A well-crafted metaphor allows us to make associations and allows our minds to craft a deeper, more lasting understanding of often complex ideas and circumstances.

As educators, we should seek ways to incorporate metaphors into our classrooms and into our daily practices. As an administrator, I use metaphors to show relationships between real-world practices and the artificial environments we often create in schools. As you read through this book, you will notice it is filled with metaphors to try and challenge your thinking. We must be willing to examine new ways to tackle old problems. If we want our students to show evidence of success unlike what they have shown before, we must be willing to explore new ways of not only thinking about things, but new ways of doing things.

I'm an avid reader. Each night, I climb into bed with a book and process my day through the lens of the written word. My dining room walls are covered with bookshelves displaying all the books I have read and the countless others on my must-read list. Teachers at my school often come to me for advice and leave with a book that I have pulled from a shelf in my office because I feel it has the answers they're looking for. Even with that, I'm comfortable saying, "I don't care if my kids choose to read."

That's a pretty big statement for a father of four, former classroom teacher, middle-school principal, elementary-school principal, and doctor of education to make. Do I really mean it? Some might think that if I do mean it, surely I don't mean I don't care if my own biological children ever pick up a book and make meaning of the text. Well for that matter, surely I don't mean the children I am asked to educate in my school. Educated adults in America would never explicitly state they don't care if their kids read. That's crazy talk.

But this career educator and father of four is saying exactly that. I don't care if my kids read, any of my kids—those who are biologically mine or those whom the public trusts me to nurture every day as a part of my profession. Does that mean I don't care about their futures? That I don't want to see my children succeed, learn, and thrive? After all, everyone will tell you that to be productive in today's society, you must be able to read. Even I agree that students should be able to read, but I think we have missed the mark by considering reading as the goal as opposed to a way to achieve a larger goal.

Perhaps we need to start using reading as a method to secure more learning instead of an isolated achievement that we then assess in isolation. Instead of saying that students who read more learn more, perhaps we should say that students who learn more read more. A slight change in word order can have profound changes on what we do. Reading is indeed a way that students can learn; however, it is not *the* way. Reading is a skill students can use to acquire more knowledge, but it is not the only way. Only when we begin to understand this can we begin to see the student achievement we are all after.

I want to change the conversation; I want educators and politicians to question what we are ultimately after and investigate new ways of achieving it. I believe we have drifted off course by focusing so much on reading, at least in the way most of us understand it—the complex skill of decoding written text to discover its meaning.

Many of us have been exposed to social studies lessons on the Protestant Reformation, which occurred during the sixteenth century. At that time, religious leaders in Europe found themselves at a crossroads. Reformers such as Martin Luther and John Calvin found themselves in the middle of controversy because of their "radical" beliefs. The basic premise of their beliefs was that common people should be able to read so they could interpret religious texts without the aid of the Catholic Church and its interpretations. This belief was so radical that it spawned wars, persecution, and the establishment of new religions. The spread of ideas through the skill of reading has been a key foundation of learning ever since.

In America during the early twentieth century, propaganda was often spread via pamphlets advertising the need for social and political unions and associations; during world wars, advertising campaigns were inspired and recruitment drives centered on well-written narratives. For the past hundred years, many Americans have started their mornings with coffee and a copy of *USA Today*, the *New York Times*, or other papers. Reading has been instrumental in the spread of ideas and has been a key to learning for hundreds of years for millions of people, so how can I say I don't care if my kids read? How will they ever become informed, productive, self-driven leaders if they do not read?

I am glad you asked.

The World Today

According to *Forbes* magazine, at the time I am writing this, the four largest publicly traded businesses in the world are based in China. As a father who wants only the best for his children, does this imply that if I want my children to be successful in this new world I should be teaching them to read and speak Chinese? Helping them learn to speak the native language of the four largest corporations in the world would surely give them a competitive advantage in securing a job. But learning Chinese is not a common practice in America.

Maybe I shouldn't worry about the flattening of the world as described by Thomas Friedman in his 2005 text, The World is Flat and should instead focus on preparing my children for their success in America by teaching them to learn English. Maybe I should discount the fact that in America over the last twenty-five years, the number of Spanish speakers and readers has nearly tripled from approximately 5 percent of the population to close to 14 percent. Or perhaps I should discount the fact that YouTube, the world's second-most popular website, averages 1 million unique visitors every month while the third-most popular site, Facebook, is close behind at 900,000 and that these sites do not focus on written text but on visual media such as photos and videos. Perhaps I should ignore the fact that state and federal authorities have increasingly reduced written text in street and traffic signs and governmental documents and forms of all types. Maybe it is inconsequential that sites such as Twitter force users to consolidate their thoughts to 140 characters or fewer while others such as Instagram and Pinterest force users to communicate with visual imagery at the expense of the written word.

We live in evolving times—a time of mass communication and social media, a time of global competition and melting-pot societies. We live in an age when information is readily available via the Internet and cable news. We live in a time when children learn to "text" (the verb, not the noun) with improper grammar and are still able to communicate well enough to get their ideas across to each other. We live in an age when talk to text, Siri, and artificial intelligence share audibly what just a few years ago required visual decoding.

Five hundred years ago, Martin Luther advocated for people to be able to read so they could acquire and interpret information independent of undue influence. Today, our children receive more information than they could ever hope to absorb. The huge question is whether they can do anything with it once they have consumed it. Have we become so focused on teaching our students how to gain fluency and gain decoding skills in written form that we have sacrificed their ability to analyze, synthesize, and evaluate information regardless of the medium that delivers it to them?

As a father and educator, I do not care if my kids read; reading is only one way they can collect information. I want my children to be able to acquire information from a variety of sources, identify the sources that provide them with the most accurate and useful information, and—most importantly—figure out what to do with it all. I want my kids doing things to learn things because when they become adults, they will be measured more by what they do than what they know.

*   *   *

Once you learn how to ride a bike, you never forget how to ride a bike. We've all heard that, right? But the educator in me wonders why it's not "Once you learn algebra [or grammar, or even mundane things such as the colors of the rainbow], you never forget." Instead, the saying wraps around a skill that is much more complex to master than memorizing a formula or frequently observed colors. Why do we have such a difficult time remembering much of anything we learned in school but never forget how to ride a bike, something most of us learned when we were five or six? Surely, it is not because the task was easy because it was anything but that, remember?

Riding a bicycle requires tremendous gross and fine motor controls, concentration, dexterity, and balance, yet it can be mastered by children before they enter school, and they will retain that skill for a lifetime. In the world of education in which we are constantly seeking the magic pill, the silver bullet that will fix everything, why haven't we studied this process and tried to incorporate it into our educational curricula at all levels? Why have we spent millions of dollars and countless hours examining strategies that continue to be proven as red herrings instead of exploring a process that has been proven to work in every country around the world?

Well, lucky for you, you have endured this reading just long enough to stumble upon what I describe as the seven-step process for achieving learning that endures. It really is as easy as learning to ride a bike.

When Cameron (my eleven-year-old son now) was still a toddler, he got his first bike—a red, blue, and yellow tricycle that had a large extension handle in the back that I could hold onto from behind and help guide and steer him with. He started learning how to pedal, maneuver the handlebars, and gain a sense of independence.

He later moved on to a larger bike with training wheels. He called it a "big kid bike"; but the training wheels helped him learn the basics of balance. It didn't take him long before he was asking me to help him ride without the training wheels. That's where the real work for the two of us started.

He and I went through some growing pains. Learning to ride a bike with only two wheels was a process. I didn't have Cameron sit on the floor in front of me while I opened up the owner's manual for his bike. I didn't read to him from an instruction booklet and then turn him loose. I didn't ask him to walk outside with me and sit at the end of the driveway and watch me model the proper technique. I didn't ride my own bike back and forth in front of him while he took notes awhile awaiting my blessing to go out and ride by himself.

What I did do was set him on his bike while holding on to the back of his seat. While he began to pedal, I began running alongside of him. We went back and forth, up and down our cul-de-sac dozens of times until I eventually got up the courage to let go. He didn't ask me to release him; I just did. And when he turned around and saw I wasn't there holding him up, he panicked. He crashed and hit the ground. I ran to him of course. But what I did not do was stand over him and declare he just wasn't a bike rider. I didn't tell him he was riding at only a four-year-old level. I picked him up, dried his tears, and told him to try again.

He and I repeated this process countless times. He of course gained confidence each time and was eventually riding on his own.

I have four kids at home, and none is alike. The experience my (currently) five-year-old Reagan went through learning to ride her bike was different. Reagan is an independent princess. Having an older brother has its drawbacks—she will never be allowed to date of course and will always be fighting for the TV remote—but it also has its perks. Reagan never rode any tricycle. She received her first training-wheel bike a month before her third birthday. When learning how to ride a big girl bike, she never required me to run alongside her; she simply needed encouragement and praise to get up when she fell down. Having a big brother to show her the ropes helped propel her forward at an earlier age. As a five-year-old, she can do some things better than Cameron did at that age. She still falls down from time to time, but her willingness to take risks and ability to do tricks is incredible for such a young girl. So how would I classify her abilities? Is she riding at an eleven-year-old level or a five-year-old level? If she had been taught this skill in school, would she have earned an A or a C? Do you need to know more about her skills to accurately assess her ability level, or is knowing that she stays upright enough to give a grade to that?

I also have two younger kids at home, neither of whom has gotten around to hopping on a bike...yet. But I have feeling that when they do, their experiences will probably also be different. I doubt they will need to follow the same routine as did their older siblings. But if they aren't bike riders by age five like their sister was, I won't panic. If they're not doing jumps and tricks at age eleven like their brother, I won't see them as struggling, delayed, and reluctant. Similarly, if they become teenagers and do not ride their bikes at all, I won't get upset because I'm sure they will have discovered other ways of entertaining themselves and getting around town. Maybe they'll ride scooters or skateboards. Maybe they'll choose to walk or run. Maybe they'll just wait until they know how to drive a car. Maybe they just won't have an interest in riding.

Ultimately, riding a bike is just one skill they can choose to learn, but it is not a requirement for being a world traveler or for becoming an adult. Who knows? Maybe in ten years, my kids will master a new method of transportation I can't even imagine today.

My point is that the ability to ride a bike is one tool they may choose to utilize. I believe being able to ride a bike would allow them to experience more and have more fun than those who don't have that ability, but it is not a requirement for experiencing more.

Being a reader—like being a bike rider—is a strategy that as an adult I can argue makes my life easier and more complete, but it would be arrogance on my part to assume that all kids should do things the same way I did as a child. Perhaps we need to focus more on the goal than on any one strategy to achieve it. As Henry Ford stated more than a century ago, "If I had asked customers what they wanted, they would have said a faster horse." Perhaps we need to be thinking outside the box we have created and focus more on the ultimate goal of helping students learn and less on forcing them to do it our way and then slapping a label on them if they choose to do so differently.

Throughout our childhoods, we probably all had varied experiences when it came to mastering the art of bike riding, but we all have some common themes. My aim in this book is to highlight some of those commonalities and to show how incorporating these into our classrooms can result in huge gains. Our goal as teachers is not to create good students but to create productive future adults. This means we cannot have as our mission to produce good test takers today if we sacrifice learning skills that will last a lifetime.

I believe we can have both—students who learn for a lifetime and are able to show evidence of their learning in the short term. We can have students who focus on life skills that will endure and manifest as high achievement scores on whatever assessment is thrown at them.

By following the seven steps outlined in this text, you'll learn that teaching students and helping them acquire learning that endures is as easy as riding a bike.

Chapter 1

Step 1: Make It Safe

When we were kids and were told to go outside and play, it wasn't uncommon for us to grab our bikes, flip the kickstands up, and just ride. We knew to be back by the time the streetlights came on and not to ride on the interstate or kill ourselves, but that was about the limit of our safe-riding guidance. We rode our bikes in the street, hopped curbs onto sidewalks, found ramps to jump, and often had the scars, scabs, and casts to prove our daring.

Today, the world is different. As news coverage on concussions and brain injuries becomes more commonplace, as states enact more-restrictive safety laws and policies, we are now in a world where buying a stylish, well-fitting helmet requires as much deliberation as buying the right bicycle. In my house, I have a daughter with a pink Disney princess helmet, a three-year-old with a helmet displaying a fake Mohawk, a blue helmet with baby ducks for my youngest, and a stylish, aerodynamic, orange-and-black helmet for my oldest child. They'll be safe when riding, and they want to look cool doing it.

Each of my kids is at a different place in his or her bike-riding progression, yet each knows that before the butts hit their seats, helmets go on heads. Before attempting to have any fun or learn any new tricks, they must be protected.

In our classrooms, the same responsibility exists. Learning needs to be safe. It needs to exist in a climate free of harm and full of security. We need to metaphorically strap our helmets on and remind our students that they will not be hurt while they're with us. We will set up procedures and processes full of feedback but free of condemnation. We will avoid sarcasm and put-downs and instead work to boost children up and increase their sense of self-worth. We will plan our instruction, and we will put just as much thought and care into making a safe learning environment as we do to making it rigorous.

We all know that some kids are more prone to injury and insult. Some kids fall down often and thus need a little more protection. I have one such child. He may need kneepads, elbow pads, and maybe even a Teflon vest to go along with his helmet when on his bike. Not every child needs that much protection, but all will need to at least protect their most vulnerable and essential component, their heads. In your classroom, you need to make sure you are also providing the same protection.

We need to be sure kids know they can grow and achieve. We need to make sure they have no fear of failure or falling. They need to know that although the learning process will be difficult and they will have stumbles, they will not get hurt and will not be harmed. We're there to make sure they are safe, protected, and secure. Students are willing to take risks and push boundaries only when they feel secure.

So how do you know if your room is safe? Quite simply, are your students willing to take chances? Does every child willingly participate? Do students try new things? Do they come to you for support? Are they willing to put their emotional, social, and academic well-being in your hands? If not, what helmets can you round up for them?

During your first two weeks of school, do you spend all your time telling your students what they can and can't do, or do you spend your time trying to establish a relationship of trust and encourage future risk taking?

My kids have all depended on me when learning to ride in part because I am convenient but in large part also because they trust that I will do them no harm. They believe that my main priority as their dad is to keep them safe. Yes, I will teach them life lessons. Yes, we will make memories. But more important, when they are with me, they feel safe. Is the same true of the students in your classroom? They may depend on you to teach them curricula and to pass out some amazing worksheets, but do they know that you will also give them challenges that are complex and dynamic and that ultimately you are there to make sure they are safe?

Think about any great relationship you have whether one with a lifelong friend, a spouse, or a family member. Your relationship was not built by establishing boundaries from the get-go but by looking for common interests, getting to know each other, sharing hopes and dreams, and making connections. If we want our classrooms to be safe places for risk taking, we must move beyond simply collecting academic achievement data on our students. We must do more than tell them all the rules and norms of our space. We must form relationships with all of them. It is only from here that we can confidently give our students the push they need to begin learning on their own. Helmets may make children feel secure, but the adults running alongside them truly makes them feel safe.

Relationships matter, but so does the environment. When learning to ride your bike, were you taken to a bumpy gravel road filled with potholes and debris, or were you guided to a flat parking lot, side street, or park? Safety is not acquired just through a helmet but also through intentionally thinking through our environments and making them suitable for risk taking. Riding a bike is a lot safer when we are on a path free of hazards and distractions. If our kids are able to focus on what is directly in front of them, if they are able to go confidently and smoothly without unnecessary bumps and distractions, the learning process they go through will be more productive.

As a teacher, what does your environment look like? Does it include metaphorical potholes and bumps that will derail students? At my school, teachers are encouraged to replicate real-world learning environments in their classrooms. When we ask our students to sit in hard student chairs behind heavy desks, stay quiet, sit in rows, and stare through ultraviolet lights, we are setting them up for failure; such an environment is not comfortable. Just as bike seats need individual adjustments, our students need to be in learning locations that fit them. Classrooms at my school are filled with beanbag chairs, palm trees, beach balls, sandboxes, couches, and recliners. When most kids leave school, they enter worlds with soft furniture, gardens, and playgrounds, so why not try to replicate that where they are preparing for real-world success? Kids tend to feel safe and secure at home. If our goal is to help students feel safe at school, why don't we try to duplicate that environment there? We need to stop trying to convince parents to set up their children's bedrooms to look like school with a quiet space, desk, and artificial light, and instead try to make our schools look like their homes. Safety and comfort go hand in hand. What can you do right now to help your students feel safe?

Just a word of advice—simply telling your students "You're safe" won't do the trick. It's up to you to create and foster the learning space, to create a climate of trust, and to promote risk taking if you want learning to take root. As you embark on the voyage of creating an environment that fosters lifelong learning, start with creating an environment of safety. Create an environment in which students depend on you to help them avoid falling yet are willing to take risks, and follow that up with creating a classroom that is comfortable and inviting for risks.

In my classroom, I offered students each one "Get Out of Jail" card per semester. So many times as teachers, we use the threat of a parent phone call to rein students in when we need to correct behaviors. In my room, I wanted my students to know that I was not just a teacher who could call home and ruin their weekends but was a man whom they could lean on to help them overcome troubles at home. Each student could submit to me a request up to two times a year to call home and celebrate an achievement with his or her parents. Students were told that they should save these phone calls for a time when they were grounded, on their parents' naughty list, or hoping for a special privilege. I'd ask my students to tell me why they needed me (verbalizing their trust in me) and what they needed me to say. Students knew I wouldn't embellish anything but would have no problem finding a strength and celebrating it.

I didn't have to make calls for every child in my classrooms to earn everyone's trust because that wasn't needed. Often, after I'd made one such call, word would spread so quickly that I gained trust "capital" with every child that would last for weeks. During these weeks, my students would do anything I asked of them because they knew I was in their corner. They would sit in their comfortable, soft seating feeling at home and knowing that we were a school family. It's all about trust. Once you have that, you have everything.

Chapter 2

Step 2: Get to the Next Driveway and Then the End of the Block Any Way You Can—Milestones and Goals

My neighborhood is made up of a series of cul-de-sacs. I live on a long, winding road, which is crossed by speed bumps, that each cul-de-sac connects to. I tend to get slightly more traffic driving past my home than do some of my neighbors who live on the dead-end streets, but the speed bumps tend to keep most drivers under control. It is on those small, closed-off, semi-private residential streets that I taught my children to ride their bikes.

Riding on my street, although more convenient, carries with it unnecessary hurdles. There is no reason a beginning bike rider should have to contend with oncoming traffic and speed bumps when a few hundred yards away is a short, straight, flat road seemingly made for them. Although riding in front of my own home is easy for me, it's not that way for my beginners.

When my kids are outside riding their bikes, they are told where to go to remain safe. When I am teaching them, I go with them. We walk our bikes to the road we want to ride on. When we arrive, we get set up and look at where we're hoping to go. We start at one end of the street, and I simply ask my children to make it to the first driveway. Then we try for the next driveway, and we eventually work our way to the end of the street. We stop and celebrate each success. I encourage their progress, and we realign our goals.

My kids knew when they were beginners that their ultimate goal was not to ride a bike down one dead-end road in one neighborhood but to eventually explore the world around them with greater ease and clarity. We had to learn and refine our skills in a safe and secure neighborhood with small measurable goals, but we knew we were doing so in an effort to apply them to the greater world and to be able to use our new skills in a way that would eventually be beneficial to them.

How does this work in your classroom? Do your students know how everything they are learning will make their lives better? Have you set small, measurable goals you can celebrate frequently? It's not enough to simply tell students that they need to learn a skill so they can pass a test or even so they can feel good about themselves. The first step in learning is about risk taking, but for our students to learn that the risks are worth their effort and discomfort, they must feel that they are making progress toward a specific goal and that their risks will have a payoff.

When you correct an assignment, do you mark how many questions a student got wrong, or do you write how many a student got correct? Do you celebrate the students who are being successful in following your routines and procedures, or do you focus your energy on those who are struggling? Do you have a way to measure progress every day and every week? Are your kids working toward a goal, a test, an event in the future when all they do is live today, or do you have a way to show them they are getting closer?

If we want our kids to succeed, we must show them that success is not a singular event but a series of events that build on each other and reach toward a goal. We make progress only by celebrating this and scaffolding our goals just as we do our instruction.

There is a reason so many kids start learning to ride with training wheels. We want them to learn the skills of balance and steering, but more important, we want them to see the value in riding a bike and feel the joy of mobility. We want them to think of themselves as bike riders. We want them to feel success. It's okay to put training wheels on your students as well as long as you have a plan for removing them. Once they come off, do you have a plan for helping them continue to see success and stay upright? The goal is independence.

My guidance and support are parts of the process, but not the final ones. When going out for our first guided lessons on the local dead-end street, each of my kids had slightly different approaches. My oldest started with training wheels, moved to more support, and then one day took off and jumped into independent riding. My daughter required me to run next to her simply cheering her on with very little physical support. My younger kids may need me to run alongside of them with a beach towel wrapped around their waists to help them balance. They may need a little more coaching and guidance. They may need less. Ultimately, they will all get to the same level of proficiency as the others although the route to that point will vary for each.

As an adult learner, I use reading as one of my primary strategies to gain knowledge, but I also know a number of adults who profess to never read; they gather their knowledge in different ways. Reading is a route to learning, but it isn't the only way just as using training wheels is just one way to learn to ride. In our classrooms, our goals should not focus on strategies but on getting students to analyze, evaluate, and create. This evaluation and analysis of ideas is what students must be able to develop. We should expose our students to a variety of information-sharing formats so we can work on these high-order skills. We can't let decoding text be our primary focus anymore; we need our students to be able to collect information and do something with it no matter where it comes from. My youngest son may need me to hold a towel around him while I run next to him as he rides, but my oldest son didn't. It would be a disservice to my kids to claim that because their routes to proficiency in bike riding were different, their ability to successfully ride today should be labeled differently. Success in a final outcome is success, no matter the route traveled to get there. In our classrooms, some children may learn from reading and some may learn from watching others, but a whole lot will learn only by doing.

Across America today, teachers are being asked to teach and assess their students based on new standards rooted in high-order thinking. Benjamin Bloom introduced his model of cognitive complexity approximately fifty years ago, and schools are just now responding to it.

When I was in elementary school, Bloom's model was more than a decade old. The problem was that my teachers were so focused on replicating their own experiences in school that they were not expected to actually apply the new theory on learning. Even today, teachers are struggling with incorporating these "new" standards because they were not expected to learn and show evidence of high-order thinking when they were in school.

Education is a vicious cycle of repeating the past to create the future. Our schools are filled with teachers who were successful when they were in school. Because they saw success back when they were students, they are doing their best to replicate that experience for their students today. Our former "A" students who were so good at memorizing and recalling information when they were kids are today asking their students to do the same thing and copy an experience instead of creating a new one.

I have had the luxury of working in half a dozen schools as a full-time educator and have visited countless others as a consultant discussing the ideas of high-order thinking, evaluation, and assessment of knowledge. In my travels from school to school, I have seen a variety of strategies and a range of successes, but I have yet to see a system-wide approach of pushing cognitive dissonance, the progressive struggle, or true critical thinking on the part of students. Even those schools that are pushing thinking forward by focusing on standards-based learning, the use of formative and summative assessment, student engagement, etc., are still missing some critical pieces as they continue to put an inordinate emphasis on reading in their master schedules, school improvement plans, and even in their teacher certification processes.

No Child Left Behind, the federal legislation that tied funding to improvements in reading, is one key reason for this. The foundation for this legislation and its related local policies is that students need to be able to access global information. Students in America need to be prepared for an evolving world and to be held to a higher standard than they were. Teachers need to be better trained so America's young people will be better prepared to be competitive in a flattening world. The focus of this legislation and many of the state initiatives that followed was on reading. This singular focus, however, may have led to some unintended consequences.

In every state in America now, schools are becoming more transparent as they are asked to publicly advertise their success on standardized tests that presume to measure student preparedness for success at the next level. Students from third to twelfth grade are assessed every year on their ability to read, and the results of these assessments determine whether a school is designated as high performing or struggling and whether it receives sanctions or praise, funding or closure. It makes sense that schools and their staffs would put such an emphasis on this singular discipline or skill set. But as a result, we may have lost sight on creating well-rounded future adults who are able to create and innovate.

We are often told that for students to learn about the world around them, they need to read more, that reading equates to more well-rounded learners. If we would just get our kids to pick up books and read, they would be so much better informed. But as schools have put such an emphasis on reading, our science and social studies scores on all standardized measures have continued to fall. As our teachers put more of a focus on reading, our kids are seemingly becoming less informed about the world around them. This is true across the country.

If you are at home in your office or in your den where you can see your bookshelf, take a look at the books on it. Do you have any books about nuclear physics? How about the breeding habits of termites? Do you have any books about the moons of Jupiter? I doubt it. I know I don't. What do you have books about? My guess is that you have books about things you are interested in and already have a basic understanding of. In my home office, I have approximately 1,000 books covering topics from the history of America to the future of society. I do not have any books about fifth-century China or how to crochet. I don't have any books about how to be a competitive cheerleader or how to distinguish a moth from a butterfly (though I am sure such books exist) because my interest in those subjects has not been sparked yet. We pick up books to enhance our knowledge; very rarely do we read to create new knowledge.

The more science and social studies we know, the better readers we will become; it's not the other way around. To create better readers, we need to make contextual associations. What we will read will be relevant to us if we have a context already established about what we are reading, and we can then begin to analyze and make inferences.

Have you ever tried to read a Dr. Seuss book to a child without showing him the pictures? Often times, the nonsense words in those books make no sense unless a child is able to see a picture to provide a point of reference. The same is true for a child picking up so many of our textbooks in school. To many, the words on the page are simply nonsense because they have no context in which to make a reference.

As a child, I picked up books about the world wars and baseball because I already had some knowledge of and interest in those subjects. I was playing baseball with my friends and hearing stories about the wars from my grandfather. If we want better readers, we actually need to put less emphasis on reading and more emphasis on learning.

In colleges of teacher education, we need future educators to learn how to facilitate learning, how to challenge students, and how to engage them in high-order thinking. We do not need teachers with a singular content focus. We need to move away from certifying teachers because they know one subject area well enough to pass a certification test; we need teachers who are learning experts not content experts. We need teachers who are able to get kids excited about learning. If we want our children to want to pick up books, we need to give them some passions. We need to make learning fun, engaging, and real.

It seems that in America today, many have bought into the idea of reading being the goal rather than a way to learning. In 2014, there were more than 300,000 books published in the United States—over 800 per day. Why do so many people write and publish texts? Hey, even I'm guilty of this. Is it really because there is that much new knowledge in the world to be shared and so many people willing to write about it, or is it is that authors feel that being published is a measure of status or accomplishment?

Regardless of their motivations, knowing that so many people from so many different experiences and knowledge bases are getting books published gives me pause because surely not all books are equally rooted in fact and accuracy. Reading some new titles may lead me astray. Before I pick up anything to read, whether it's the Sunday newspaper or a popular new novel, I need to be sure I am prepared to analyze the words on the page so I can make informed inferences and not just take the written word at face value. Too many people in this world have been led astray by doing just that. It's not always as notorious as a Facebook creeper or a malicious help-wanted ad, but the approach is the same. If you are not able to distinguish between fact and fiction, if you are not able to determine intent and motive, if you are not able to effectively analyze and evaluate what you're reading, your life can change in an instant. The good news is that reading is not the only strategy for learning. Our kids today know this. It's about time we educators figure this out as well.

Here is a small challenge to help confirm this point. I don't want you to accept my words as true simply because you're reading them; that would go against everything I'm trying to explain. Here's what I want you to do. When you finish this chapter (don't do it now; you need a little background first), try this and see what you discover. Put this book down and turn on your TV. Channel surf a bit to see what's being broadcast and decide which shows caught your interest. Be mindful of the fact that for some reason, you have decided to forgo TV watching right now to read, but assume that you wanted to watch TV. Would you want to watch every show on, or would you be selective based on your tastes and interests? Would you watch a sporting event or a cooking show? Would you choose a cable news program over a sitcom? How would you decide what to watch?

We watch TV shows that intrigue and excite us. Why do we expect it to be any different with our reading habits? I have messed up on this with my own kids. I've told them at times to turn off the TV and pick up a book. "Which one?" they'd ask, and I'd say, "I don't care. Just go read." They may have been watching something together that they were enjoying—maybe something on the Disney Channel they all agreed to watch after some give-and-take negotiations with each other. They may have been learning much-needed social skills that I interrupted by sending them off to read books individually and as a result learned nothing new. Not all TV is bad. Bad TV is bad. Likewise, not all reading is good. Good reading is good.

Concerning the 300,000 books published this year, odds are that very few will ever be considered classic by future generations. Very few will make their authors any money or give them platforms for educating and informing others. Not every movie is a blockbuster, and not every book hits the best-seller lists. Our goal has to go beyond textual fluency and comprehension. We must strive for literacy: information literacy, media literacy, textual literacy, and so on. We need to help our students learn how to learn, and we need to realize learning happens in a variety of ways. Though reading is a helpful tool for me, I don't care if my kids choose to read—I want them to learn. Learning to read may be the metaphorical equivalent of riding to the first driveway with training wheels on, but it is not our goal. It's not the same as a ride through the neighborhood hopping curbs, creating new stunts, and seeing new sites. It is one way to get closer to independence but not the only way.

I was once scrolling through my Twitter feed and saw an insightful phrase: "Bloom's Taxonomy—the most often quoted research in education that nobody has actually read." We live in an age ruled by platitudes and generalities. We hear a sweeping declaration and assume it must be true. We can look at Facebook any night of the week and read about the latest teacher who is destroying math as we know it by embracing common-core math and actually teaching students why numbers make sense and not just teaching students to memorize formulae. We turn on the TV at night and realize that most young adults are getting their news from Comedy Central, not from a major network. We watch election campaigns where candidates speak with passion and anger but rarely voice an agenda or innovation.

The inability to determine fact from fiction, opinion from information, is not just an issue for our kids; we adults are not immune to this. We get sucked into the same trap as do the kids we're trying to teach. We argue that we want our students to make informed decisions based on logic and reasoning, yet we get fooled by following mass media and popular, often unfounded, opinion. Then we go into our classrooms and teach our students to do the same thing.

We scold students who copy off their peers but celebrate them when they copy off us. We ask students to learn the skills of collaboration but then ask them to simply do what we do and believe what we say. As adults, we thrive on convenience and ease. We live busy lives and want our pizzas delivered, our groceries bagged, our money direct deposited, our retirement accounts managed, our cable, Internet, and phone bundled, and our lives to be directed by others. But we would never say that aloud because after all, we are a nation of independent thinkers and innovators. We are educators of the next generation of inventors and engineers, and if our students would just do what we said and how we said it, they would learn to think for themselves. For those of you who may still be taking this text at face value, that was sarcasm.

It is ideal to say that 100 percent of our students will achieve, but having teachers commit to reaching 100 percent of their students all the time is asking for immovable and inflexible teachers. I tend to stick to the rule of eighty. I ask teachers to commit to reaching 80 percent of their kids on 80 percent of the standards they have signed off on. Imagine being a ninth-grade teacher who inherits a child who has been in the district since kindergarten. If each teacher in the system agreed to ten standards a year (one per month) per subject area to teach to mastery (power standards), as a ninth-grade teacher, you could look back and identify at least ninety standards this child has been exposed to, and hopefully, this child will be proficient in at least seventy-two (80 percent) of them.

When you calculate how this adds up by subject area per year, the learning that takes place in the mind of a child is really exponential. Students are no longer learning isolated facts that have little relevance. Each year, teachers are building on prior conceptions and taking learning to greater depths.

In our classrooms, we must work to identify our goal. We must identify and articulate to our students where their learning will take them. There's nothing wrong with introducing any strategy for achieving success, but we can get lost in the process. We must determine when students are making progress and make adjustments when they aren't. If we continue to lock ourselves into only one way of doing and leaning anything, we will continue to stifle creativity and inadvertently designate some kids as failures when the reality may be that they just haven't found success yet or in the way we would have done it.

Let's open our minds and look for ways to allow every child to succeed and grow even if that means humbling ourselves and acknowledging that our way is not the only way. We must set our goals on life goals. We don't just want our kids riding to the next driveway. If we want them riding all over the neighborhood, eventually we need to let them go and not get hung up on how they ride, just the fact that they do.

Chapter 3

Step 3: Help Them Achieve Balance and Create Momentum

Whenever I was sick as a child and would stay home from school, I'd watch Bob Barker host *The Price is Right*. I loved watching contestants spin the big wheel hoping to win big bucks. Some of the big, strong men would send the wheel spinning and almost falling off its axis. Some frail women would almost lose their balance when they spun the wheel and would get at most one revolution if that. Getting that big push to create momentum was hard for them but extremely entertaining for me to watch.

As my kids have learned to ride their bikes, I have discovered the same truth. The hardest part for each of them has always been figuring out how to spin the pedal around once to overcome their inertia without my assistance. When they were beginners, it was my job to eliminate that hurdle so they could get on to pedaling; I learned that the first push can actually be the last thing they acquire. There was no reason it had to get in the way of acquiring other skills. Forcing them to learn something in a prescribed order simply because my arrogance told me it had to be done that way may have actually impeded their overall success.

Instead, I held the bike as they climbed on. I grabbed the bike seat and pushed them forward after their feet were on the pedals. Once they got moving, I'd encourage them to pedal. The initial push I provided was to help them get going and to allow that momentum to enhance their ability to balance. The initial push was my responsibility; if I had left it to them to acquire that ability by themselves, they could have crashed and fallen and perhaps would have ended up scared of riding.

Aside from bike riding with my kids, one of my passions is running. It's therapeutic for me in that it allows me to push my limits and stay healthy at the same time. Sometimes when I am speaking with educators, I make analogies comparing student learning to going for a run. There are similarities—both involve goal setting, measuring progress, and motivation. As a matter of fact, that metaphor is actually the centerpiece for most of my talks. However, there is at least one place where this metaphor falls apart and where bike riding paints a better picture.

On Saturday mornings, I go for my longest run of the week. I typically log between ten and fifteen miles on those runs on the white, sandy beaches in Florida and often go over a bridge in the process. Runners often debate what they would rather do—run uphill or downhill. I'd rather run uphill. Running uphill is taxing on my muscles, but that's about it. When I run downhill, my knees hurt, my ankles throb, my back hurts, and my whole body tenses. I know it may seem bizarre, but I consider running uphill easier than running downhill. But that's not the case when riding a bike. Every bike rider will tell you that downhills are where the fun is. You can stop pedaling and still pick up speed.

I have seen far too many teachers generating lessons that require students to climb a hill before coasting down it, the fun part. We make them put forth tremendous effort, and some give up before reaching the summit and experiencing the joy of the downhill glide.

What if we would turn that around? What if we helped kids start at the top of a hill, give them a gentle push down, and let them experience the rush of speed and adrenaline that can then carry them at least in part up the next hill?

In our classrooms, we must embrace the belief in momentum. Don't make kids plow through worksheets, textbooks, and tests just to eventually get to a fun, engaging activity. Don't subscribe to the belief that students have to earn the right to have fun and make their learning relevant. It's our responsibility to make learning a downhill glide. Hook them early. Get them to enjoy the ride, and let their momentum carry them through the work. Doing this backward just convinces kids and bike riders that it's just not worth the effort.

On a similar note, momentum has to be sustained. If you sit still on a bike, you'll fall over. Don't allow your kids to sit still waiting for the next action-packed moment. Once you have them moving, keep them moving. Stopping anytime will force you to start the process all over. If you have the hill on the backside of your lessons, don't waste it by not planning for continuing the process—keep them moving.

Just as I've not forced my children to make the initial push of the pedal, in our classrooms, we must do all we can to eliminate our own teacher preferences. We often lose sight of our goal and instead put other roadblocks in front of our kids in an attempt to do what we think is right. I don't make my kids start by pedaling; I also don't make them ride over speed bumps and potholes. It's important for my kids to learn how to pedal independently, but that doesn't have to be taught first. I never explicitly taught it to either of my oldest kids; they just picked it up themselves as they decided to take their learning to a more independent level, and they became more daring, ambitious, and confident.

Let me mix metaphors again. Imagine I'm an administrator in your school who tells you that running is therapeutic and offers health benefits. I tell you that if you take up running, you'll be a highly effective teacher free from stress who has to take few if any sick days. I say that you as a teacher must be a runner if you want your evaluation to reflect your capabilities. Not just any runner though. You must run as much as I do because I consider myself a successful educator and running is something I have done to get where I am. It works for me, so it must work for you. I tell you that I expect you to run a marathon at the end of the school year. If you complete it, I'll consider you an effective teacher who has passed the test. If you don't, I'll consider you ineffective and as having failed.

We all know this would never fly in any school in America; it would result in a grievance being filed. I have no right to tell teachers that to be successful teachers they have to run marathons. For starters, I have no evidence other than my own experience, to say there is a correlation between completing marathons and being a good teacher. Second, it just wouldn't be fair. Some of my teachers may have never run a day in their lives. Perhaps a PE teacher might get excited about this, but how about a teacher who's just had a knee replacement?

My final evaluation of you as a teacher should focus on what really matters—student success and growth—I shouldn't get caught up in evaluating my own biased opinion of what is important. How often do we do this in our own classrooms though? How often do we tell students that they must pedal before they ride? That they must run to succeed? That they must write in cursive? That they must read the book, not watch the movie? That they must learn something by Friday? That they must use a Venn diagram and not their own picture graphs?

Learning happens at different times in different ways and in different forms. When we make kids jump through our hoops, we can inadvertently stop their momentum, cause them to fall off the bike, and lose sight of the goal—future independence. As the guide to their learning, we have to do all we can to provide the initial push for them if that's necessary, but we ultimately have to just get out of their way. If we want bike riders, we should do all we can to teach bike-riding skills. Riding a bike is the goal to be evaluated, not the process for getting there.

The same is true in your classroom. Figure out what your goal is and do whatever you can to get the kids there. Measure their progress, not their process. There is a difference.

Chapter 4

Step 4: Pick Them Up When They Fall

All bike riders, even experienced riders, will take tumbles. We can have help with pushes to get us going, and we can learn to balance ourselves, but we will all at some time fall. It's guaranteed. We fall down when learning to ride. We fall down when we do stunts and tricks. We fall down when we are making millions of dollars and creating YouTube videos or competing in the X Games, but those who get better don't stay down long; they get back up.

As kids experiment with new things, they will experience hardships. They will fall. They will get hurt. They will make mistakes. As much as we try to prevent it, it will happen. We don't help them fall, but it's our responsibility to help them get up. We reach out loving hands, dry their tears, and celebrate how far they've come. We inspire, we motivate, we push, we teach. We don't label. We don't limit.

When my children fall, I don't stand over them and tell them they've failed. I don't label them as "not a bike rider" or someone who should stick to walking. I help them up. I nurture the bruised knees and bruised egos and encourage them to try again.

Learning is all about do-overs. Doing anything right the first time is not a sign of learn-ing but a sign of learn-ed. We need to allow for mistakes. We must allow for slips and falls and not allow them to be judgments or inhibitors of future success. When my daughter falls off her bike on the first day she is trying or the tenth day she is trying, it has no bearing on whether she will be a bike rider three weeks later. I don't tell her she is only partly a bike rider because she'd fallen off earlier. The fact that she can ride today is all that matters. Falling happens, but soon after, so does success.

Our classrooms are places of learning. As such, our students are going through an often messy process toward acquiring skills. They will fall down as they go. The question is, what do we do about it? Do we label them as failures when they fall? Do we give condemning progress updates, or do we uplift, inspire, and encourage perseverance?

How does your feedback look in your class? In most classrooms, the primary mechanism by which we communicate progress to students is through grading. The standards-based grading movement is one that has caught a lot of traction in recent years. It centers on the idea of identifying concrete and specific standards of learning and ensuring that students' grades reflect the evidence that has been observed in relation to student mastery of that standard. Most of the teachers I have worked with across the country are able to understand the need for concrete, descriptive feedback, but they struggle with how that feedback manifests itself in a child in the learning process. Learning is very rarely binary; there is no light bulb that turns on in our minds when we all of a sudden learn something new. Learning has a slide dimmer that gradually increases the amount of light we see as our neurons make new connections. Being a bike rider is not a "Yes you are" or "No you're not" proposition either. How would one differentiate standards-based feedback based on whether a child can ride with one hand on the handlebars or two? Is a child relying on training wheels more proficient than a child with a parent holding onto the seat? Is a child riding a unicycle more advanced than an adult riding a motorcycle?

In our classrooms, we often have a wide range of skills and abilities. We know all our students are at different places in their learning progression and will make mistakes as they learn. Do we allow for that, or do we expect every child to show the same skills in the same way at the same time without error? If we are in the learning business, it's time we begin to get into the business of embracing mistakes.

Let's start this discussion with a few practical yet powerful strategies. In your classroom, when students make mistakes, do they get the opportunity to redo whatever task, assignment, or activity was expected for full credit? Do you collect every assignment students submit, those with multiple mistakes as well as those with few or no mistakes, provide grades, and calculate an average score based on the mean? If so, why?

When I see Bs on my children's report card, do I know if they struggled early in the process or later? Do I know what they struggled with or excelled in? Do I know if they understood the content but struggled with turning assignments in on time or at all? We use grades to communicate with our parents and our students, but as I am told often, if people do not understand what I am saying, I am not communicating very well. It's on me to figure out a better way to get my point across.

The same is true in your classroom. If we are to encourage risk taking, we cannot penalize failure. We cannot include initial struggles in a final grade if progress was eventually made. Using the running metaphor from earlier, if I trip on a curb running tomorrow morning and spend ten minutes nursing my injury but in three weeks run a race and come in third place, my medal will not be stripped from me because of my mistake in practice. Is the same thing true in your classroom?

Students must learn that mistakes are not opportunities for condemnation. Mistakes will not have a negative impact on them but will actually allow them to succeed in the future. If that's the case, we have to stop telling students that they have only one chance to get it right, that they cannot try again. We have to stop averaging student work by giving the same weight to first attempts as we do final attempts. Our job as educators is to provide enduring knowledge today and prepare students for success in the future.

I have heard the argument that the real world does not allow redos and retakes so as teachers we shouldn't. Actually, adults get to redo failed marriages by marrying again. Adults can leave jails after serving time and reenter the workforce and civilized society. All high-stakes standardized tests—the ACT, the SAT, the GRE— allow for multiple attempts, retakes, and redos. Allowing for do-overs is what we do our entire life. It is often only in our classrooms that we discourage this, and usually, our rationale has nothing to do with learning. We discourage it for our convenience or due to our arrogance or misguided beliefs that we are teaching some sort of social lesson that doesn't need to be taught.

We allow our kids to hop back on their bikes once they fall down; we allow toddlers to get back on their feet after stumbling when learning to walk. Why do we feel the need in our classrooms to limit opportunities for success and to hold initial failures and struggles against a child? Struggles and failures are opportunities for feedback and improvement. They cannot and should not be opportunities for labels and indictments.

A few years ago, I heard something that has stuck with me. Imagine you're teaching three people how to pack parachutes and you test them weekly during your six-week course. Here are the grades you've given them each week.

Student A: 95, 75, 82, 45, 35, 40
Student B: 62, 62, 62, 62, 62, 62
Student C: 40, 35, 45, 82, 75, 95

Which of these students one do you want packing your chute? Average all the grades and you get 62 for each student, a D in most classrooms today. But does that reflect what happened during the six weeks?

Student C is the student most would say they want packing their chute. That makes complete sense if they're planning on jumping from a plane at the end of the six-week course. But what if they were faced with jumping at the end of week 1? Would their answer change? Based on these scores, we could argue that Student C has shown the most growth and has finally demonstrated he has learned this critical skill. His early struggles shouldn't be used against him. Student B's substandard grades never changed. Student A may have known this skill all along and just got tired of the weekly performance checks. The bottom line is, your grades should not be an average of struggles and successes. It should reflect what is current and accurate—that will give you the clearest story and the best feedback.

Here's a challenge for your classroom. If you must give cumulative grades, count the most recent evidence a student gives you and simply provide feedback on prior attempts. Allow and encourage students to redo and improve initial attempts. We do it often in writing classes with rough drafts and final drafts. We need to encourage the same thing in all classes. When students make mistakes, remind them of the power of "yet." They will ultimately learn it if they persist. Only by falling do we learn to get back up.

Still not convinced that retakes and redos are a natural part of adult life? I'm currently in my seventeenth year as a public-school educator. I have been a middle-school teacher, a director of gifted programming, a coach, a dean, an assistant principal, and a principal. I have worked in four districts and two states. I have traveled to almost every state in America presenting and collaborating and have met some amazing people. I have been blessed by my opportunities, yet I still have a drive for more, a drive that sometimes makes me do some pretty stupid things. In 2003, I made some costly mistakes.

That year, I graduated with a master's in educational leadership. That was only three years after I started my career as a teacher, and I was already a certified "leader" in education. After three years, I knew I had all the answers, and I was ready to be the next great leader in the world of public education. I was ready to jump in, get a title as an administrator, and start guiding my teachers to change everything they were doing and start copying my way of teaching so they would all see great success. After all, we all know leadership is just a title and once you get the title, people immediately respect you and want to do everything you say. (Again, more sarcasm.) In 2003, I went on fourteen job interviews seeking either an assistant principal or a school principal position being sure somebody would hire a young administrator who obviously knew it all.

After visiting fourteen schools and meeting with fourteen committees, I received zero job offers. What? I was sure I was the next best thing to happen to schools. I knew it; after all, I'd been a successful student. I had worked as a teacher for three years basically copying all the techniques of the best teachers I'd had over the years, and my students were getting great grades assigned by me. I considered my total lack of job offers a major injustice and a disservice to the students those fourteen districts were paid to educate, or so I thought.

I was used to standing in front of 150 kids every day who expected me to have the answer to everything. I was paid to have the most knowledge in the room. I was definitely smarter than all my twelve-year-olds. I proved it every day by shutting down all their "disrespect" for questioning my sound logic and debating my reasoning. These twelve-year-olds had no right to question my authority and my intelligence by asking for clarity or seeking new ways of answering old problems. I was a master teacher who had no patience with preteens who questioned why the world worked as it did. If they just listened to what I was telling them, they would learn all they needed to know.

In the fall of 2003, after facing a summer of rejections, I decided to prove to everyone just how smart I was. With so many doors to school administration positions being slammed shut in front of me, I decided to try my hand at law school and really put my intelligence to the test. After all, everyone knows doctors and lawyers are the smartest people around, and I was so much more than "just" a teacher, so why not join the ranks of the elites?

The fall of 2003 was one of the most humbling seasons of my life. Law school was like no school I had ever been in before. Law school required me to think and answer questions that had no answers. My professors spent very little time giving me statistics and data; they spent the bulk of their time asking me questions; I considered the Socratic method as torture. I was good at playing school, but law school was a struggle. I had passed my GRE and LSAT exams with ease, but I was having difficulty in an environment in which I was being asked to think for myself. I was expected to read cases, legislation, and interpretations and evaluate texts and ideas through my own lens looking for errors, omissions, lapses in judgment, or causes for celebration. My professors were not doing school as I had always experienced it and had always proven myself successful at. They were doing all they could to question my thinking and challenge me to reflect and develop a sense of analysis and evaluation that I had never before had to the degree they were demanding.

Looking back on it now, I am thankful that I was not given a leadership position prior to my experience in law school. I probably would have worked tirelessly to simply create schools similar to those I'd been in, schools that worked well for kids who knew how to play school, schools that were good at creating future teachers but struggling to live up to their mission of creating lifelong learners.

Thirteen years later, I now see the proverbial light that is not a focused laser but one that contains the whole spectrum of colors. My professional goal is to help educators question what they do and why they do it. My goal is not to judge or condemn but to help them focus on their intentionality.

In your classroom, are you working to create thinkers or students who can repeat every word you say and every text you ask them to read? Are you trying to help create kids who can describe the way the world was or kids who can help create the world to be? In a world in which more than 300,000 books are published every year, we need to educate a population that does not thrive just on the knowledge available in texts. We cannot have our students pick up books, sit in our classrooms listening to us, and expect them to know all they need to know to be successful in the world they will inherit. We need to teach them how to learn in a variety of ways and contexts for a variety of reasons. We need to teach our students how to process information from social media, their peers, politicians, and digital media as well as from print media. We need to teach our students how to go beyond recall, remembering, and understanding information to get them to a point that they're analyzing, evaluating, and creating information.

We teachers have to learn to do exactly that first. We need to guide the process, to model it, or at least to enable it. That's what this book is about. True learning, lasting learning is not about copying the thoughts of others; it's about feeling safe enough to strike out on our own and create something new, powerful, and original. Let's get our kids comfortable enough to take risks, to fail miserably, and to get back up and try again.

Chapter 5

Step 5: Cheer Them On

When I was a student teacher in the suburbs of Detroit, I endured some minor hazing. It was nothing like what happens in fraternity houses and locker rooms; it was instead more of an initiation into the ranks of teachers. I was asked to be a part of every committee and coach every sport, and one Friday afternoon, I was told to dress up in a skirt and wig to play the part of a passionate cheerleader rooting kids on to success during a homecoming pep rally. As a twenty-two-year-old male fresh out of college, I had no problem with being a little crazy, but I didn't realize that wearing that outfit and playing the part of a hyper and overly hairy cheerleader would become a metaphor for my teaching throughout my career.

I absolutely love teaching—it's my calling, my passion, and my mission not because I love everything I teach but because I love every*one* I teach. Teaching is hard work. The planning, grading, reflecting, meeting, and collaborating never seem to end, but I love it!

Parenting is the same way. Whenever I tell people I have four kids, they say, "Wow! You must be busy." The truth is that I was busy when I had just one kid. I'd be busy if I had ten. Being a parent does mean you are busy, but I wouldn't trade it for the world.

As a parent, I do all I can to carve out individual time for each of my kids to spend with me. I want them to know I value them as individuals and they are important to me. I want to be at their soccer and baseball games and dance recitals. I want to support them in everything. I want them to know I will be their guide, their support, and their lifelong teacher. I want to be the one to teach them how to tie their shoes, brush their teeth, and ride their bikes. All children need cheerleaders who push them beyond what they can do now to accomplish something new tomorrow.

There is a reason universities and high schools have cheerleading programs. Cheerleaders, beyond building their own individual skills and team mind-sets, help develop an overall culture of optimism and hope. Cheerleaders instill hope about what's possible even when their teams are losing. Their job is to rally the troops and get them back up. When my children are learning anything new, that's my responsibility as well. When they're wobbling on their bikes, when they fall, when they think it's too hard, my job is to encourage them not to give up. I'd never say, "You know, some people are just walkers and others are bike riders. Maybe you're just a walker." I try to inspire them and let them know that persistence and practice will see them through temporary setbacks.

How many times have you heard teachers tell students, "You know, math isn't for everyone" or "Some people are just not creative"? Our job as teachers is to remind our students that learning is hard, that it's a struggle if done right. It will cause bruises and humble them, but it can be done. Our job is to pick all our students up, show them their individual potentials, and convince them to keep their eyes on the goal, not the struggle they're currently enduring. Our job is to use current circumstances to come up with a game plan for future success.

You can read countless studies on the dangers of labeling kids. As a teacher who spent several years teaching children identified as "at risk" as well as children labeled as "gifted", I know children will embrace whatever labels are placed on them. I have had struggling students state that they couldn't do this or that simply because in the past, an adult had told them they couldn't. I've had gifted students say they weren't supposed to ever struggle again because of what they had been told to believe about themselves.

Kids will always live up to our expectations when they know what they are. If your children are not persisting and finding success however you describe it, odds are the fault is not with them. Either you haven't made your expectations known or you have and your expectations are that they won't succeed.

Get in the habit of cheering your children on. Success breeds success; it's the most contagious virus in school. Find something small and cheer it. You will be surprised how that one victory leads to the accomplishment of so much more.

Using a rubric of learning is a step in the right direction. Rubrics have been around in education for decades. Many times, teachers hear the word *rubric* and read that as *grade requirements*. They create a checklist of tasks or directions and give students points based on their ability to jump through hoops and create projects that meet their specifications. Maybe a child will earn ten points for having a picture on the poster board. Perhaps spelling and grammar are worth another ten points on the assignment and having relevant information in a poster presentation is worth thirty points. A child completes a project and presents information to the class while the teacher holds onto a rubric in the back of the room and assigns a grade of thirty-five out of fifty because, although the student demonstrated a thorough understanding of the content, she may not have had a colorful picture and may have misspelled a few words. The student gets a 70, a C–.

In my classes, I always followed the rule of eighty, that is, 80 percent of my kids have to earn an 80 percent or better before I felt the class had mastered a topic. According to my rule of eighty, this child, who demonstrated understanding of the content, would not have been considered proficient (reaching 80 percent) just because she did not color in a picture and misspelled a word or two. Something about that doesn't seem right.

I know we have to get kids used to paying attention to the details and following directions and rules. I have no problem with holding my students accountable for almost anything I feel is important, but I must decide if they understood what I presented, if I have to reteach it, and who is ready for something new. My rule of eighty was my mechanism for making such instructional decisions, but it required that my grades all mean something—that they were all aligned and measured the same things, and most of the time coloring was not something I was focused on teaching.

A teacher can try to rely on her memory of all her 120 students and every interaction she had with each one, but inevitably, somebody or some encounter will be forgotten. Instead, to make informed decisions, she decides to take a quick look at the grades in her gradebook to determine if her students are learning. Only if her grades are accurate measures of success will this approach work.

Like most teachers she finds zeroes to hundred throughout her gradebook. These numbers do absolutely nothing to guide her teaching. She has no clue if any one day was a good or bad day. Even that score of seventy out of hundred doesn't do much. Later, she can't remember if the child had a great colorful picture and a perfect presentation in terms of syntax but missed the content, or if the child demonstrated mastery of the material but had experienced some missteps with its presentation. Perhaps the subject matter contained a number of smaller essential concepts that required varying degrees of understanding. As the teacher, she needs to know what each child knows and doesn't and to what extent. Her grades should help her make informed decisions about what she needs to do to help each child progress from where he or she is. If not, her ability to make student-centered instructional decisions will be limited and she will find herself making decisions out of convenience and just doing what she thinks is best based on instinct. Somehow, she must find a new way.

Lucky for you, there is a new way based on the same rubric system many of you are already familiar with. Unlike the rubrics most teachers are accustomed to that are focused on evaluating a task, I use rubrics to assess learning, not compliance. A rubric of learning is not task specific. If developed correctly, a rubric of learning can be used on an infinite number of tasks and have a simple purpose—determine student understanding and growth. They are not created to judge and assign a grade but to diagnose and provide prescriptive information. Rubrics of learning serve as tools for the practitioner and provide feedback to the learner.

Below is a template for what one of these rubrics might look like. If it makes perfect sense to you, feel free to stop reading here, get into your classroom, and start implementing it. Others might like a little explanation.

Standard:

_____
_____
_____

List the content students need to know (nouns/objects of the standard) along the left column of the below chart.

Identify the verb of the standard and this becomes your level 3/proficient level of the standard.

Levels "1" and "2" become lower level skills on Blooms. Level "4" is a higher order skill on Blooms.

This rubric should not be task dependent, but should assess learning.

	1 (not quite)	**2** (almost)	**3** (got it)	**4** (advanced)

In my schools, teachers are asked first to determine what their primary focus will be. We go through an exhaustive process of determining leverage, endurance, and the need for standards to identify standards of focus that we call power standards (more on this later).

These rubrics come into play once you as the teacher have selected your ten to fifteen power standards for the year. You know different kids learn in different ways at different times and with different styles. You know that each standard you have is complex and sometimes difficult to understand. You know that great teachers are able to take complex concepts and simplify them by breaking them down. Your job is to move your students wherever they are to a point of greater understanding. You also have to document where your kids are at all times so you can make informed, student-centric decisions. You know that because kids learn in different ways, there is also the reality that they can display their understanding of content in different ways. The rubric of learning is a great starting point for incorporating all this.

In the template provided, I use a four-point scale, which is helpful for many reasons but not essential. You can use any number of points as long as they are consistently applied to every standard. Many schools already do a variation on this by converting letter grades into number grades, usually on a four-point scale (think g.p.a). This does away with the need for letter grades and translations of them that can be interpreted in different ways by so many people, and it allows the learner and the teacher to see a simple, quantifiable assessment of understanding.

The primary purpose for a four-point rubric is not to assign a grade or labeling its recipients as successes or failures; it's about assessing current understanding and diagnosing prescriptive instruction. It allows us to inspire future success rooted in a current reality. It allows us to play cheerleader, to look at a scoreboard and remind a student that the game is not done yet.

Twenty years ago, when you'd take your car to a mechanic, you would let a mechanic bang around under the hood until he was able to create an invoice for a dozen emergencies that had to be addressed for a few hundred dollars. Not being an expert in automobile mechanics, you were forced to take his word for it and write the check. Nowadays, cars are equipped with diagnostic computers. A trip to a mechanic now involves your car getting hooked up to a computer that within a few minutes can pinpoint mechanical issues. At that point, just the issue or issues that need to be fixed are addressed, saving you time and money. The same process is at play when a rubric of learning is utilized. As a teacher, using a rubric of learning allows you to pinpoint what needs to be addressed and what is already working, saving you valuable time and resources.

Let's walk through a fictitious example. Let's assume you have a standard that reads, "Students will be able to apply the principles of balance, coordination, gross motor skills, and dexterity to successfully ride a bike." I'm using a fictitious example because I know how critical it is for you to work through the real standards on your own and with your peers. That struggle and conversation you will have is a part of the process of learning the standards.

In our example, with a four-point scale, the teacher (you) would look at the standard and identify the verb, in this case, *apply*. It is assumed that this step was already completed during the decision-making process of selecting this standard as one of our power standards. We know that by looking at that one verb, all our students will be asked to produce evidence that shows they can apply some new knowledge. In a four-point rubric, we use our level 3 column to detail that standard performance expectation, so the word *apply* is filled in throughout.

	1 (Not Quite)	2 (Almost)	3 (Got it)	4 (advanced)
			APPLY ...	
			APPLY ...	
			APPLY....	
			APPLY....	

Application is our standard goal for all kids for this standard, but we understand that not all students will be at this required depth at the same time. It isn't adjusted because a student may have a label or come to us with a deficit. The label may help us select our instructional approach, but remember, a standard is standard only if it's standard. Different kids will begin with different levels of understanding, but being proficient in a standard should not be measured with a sliding scale. An inch is an inch on every ruler. It is standard. Using Bloom's Taxonomy as a guide (you may also choose to use Webb's Depth of Knowledge if you're more comfortable with it), a level 2 would contain a verb with a lower level of complexity, and a level 1 would be even simpler. In this example, a level 2 may involve showing an understanding of the essential concept, and a level 1 may be as low level as recall. The rubric allows the teacher to identify what depth of understanding a student is able to demonstrate evidence of and then to pinpoint future instruction. A more detailed explanation of how to understand depth of understanding, or high-order thinking if you prefer that description, is provided later in this book (see the chapter titled "My Own Experience").

	1 (Not Quite)	2 (Almost)	3 (Got it)	4 (Advanced)
	RECALL...	UNDERSTAND ...	APPLY ...	
	RECALL...	UNDERSTAND ...	APPLY ...	
	RECALL...	UNDERSTAND ...	APPLY....	
	RECALL...	UNDERSTAND ...	APPLY....	

Detailing the verbs (the student expectation) for the first three levels on the rubric is always the first things to do on a rubric. If you can identify the verb from the standard, you simply move backward down Bloom's Taxonomy to represent lower levels of understanding. There are numerous cheat sheets available online to help you determine the basic flow of verb complexity. A generalized summary looks something like: recall, understanding, application, analysis, synthesis, evaluation, and creation.

The next step is to articulate the "what" of the standard. Each standard describes an action and the content that students will have to create evidence of. In our example, there are four explicitly stated subjects: balance, coordination, gross motor skills, and dexterity. As a teacher, you may choose to break these concepts down even further to gather greater prescriptive information, but for our purposes, we will just use those four that are listed on the first column on our rubric and measure them as we assess student understanding.

	1 (Not Quite)	2 (Almost)	3 (Got it)	4 (advanced)
Balance	RECALL...	UNDERSTAND...	APPLY ...	
Coordination	RECALL...	UNDERSTAND...	APPLY ...	
Gross motor skills	RECALL...	UNDERSTAND...	APPLY....	
Dexterity	RECALL...	UNDERSTAND...	APPLY....	

In the above example, I haven't provided great amounts of detail in each cell. For example in column 1, we see only recall ... balance. As the teacher, you may decide that the student needs to be able to recite from memory the definition of balance, simply match the proper definition of balance from a list of options, or do other basic recall functions. How you as the teacher or student demonstrate this is not of the utmost importance; this column in this rubric deals with a student's ability to remember basic information. The format of the assessment is not critical. Differentiation is key, but this is all about learning to measure a variety of tasks presented in many ways so the measurements actually help inform future decision making.

I am not offering a magic pill here; what matters is your ability to measure student learning and its depth. The formatting of the assessment at levels 1 and 2 are almost inconsequential; it isn't our goal to get a child to be successful at level 1. Our goal is to get them to at least level 3.

Let me add one more caveat; moving to a greater depth of understanding is not the same as working toward harder work. These rubrics do not move a child from easy to hard; instead, they measure depth. As a former social studies and language arts teacher, I admit I'm horrible at memorizing dates or spelling words correctly. These skills involve low-level recall but are nonetheless very difficult for me. If I am given dates or words on a page and asked to draw comparisons, to analyze, or to apply information at a greater depth, I can do that a lot easier on most topics than if I am asked to memorize information I may regard as trivial. What I can do is not necessarily harder work, but it indicates a deeper understanding.

The same is often true with kids learning to ride bikes. The hardest work tends to be done when they are building their foundations of balance and coordination. As they advance and show greater skills, they may actually be doing work that is more complex and dynamic but may not necessarily be harder.

Teachers assessing students' knowledge with one of these rubrics don't have to first evaluate whether students can perform level 1 skills before evaluating their ability to demonstrate levels 2 and 3. I argue that it should be done in reverse. Because these rubrics are to be used as diagnostic tools, a teacher should begin by measuring if a student is proficient at the standard level, level 3. If so, then there is no need to measure the levels below. Only when a student is unable to perform at a level consistent with the standard should a teacher assess what a child can do and understands because that will provide the foundation for future instruction and allow the teacher to know where to begin tomorrow.

But what about students who are able to show proficiency earlier than their peers? In the past, teachers would use such students to help teach others thinking that that would help them understand the material better. This may be true, but most teachers had no way to prove it, nor was it always fair for the students. Just because certain children have a better grasp of a concept should not mean they are given more work and the responsibility of bringing up others who are struggling. As teachers, our responsibility is to help all children grow including those who may be moving quicker than others. A four-point rubric gives us some guidance on how to do this.

Once students have demonstrated that they have a grasp of the minimum standard by achieving a level 3, you as the teacher must decide what's next. Although the best teachers are those who possess bold humility—a realization of their power to change a life yet a willingness to realize they do not have all the answers—arrogant teachers are those who believe the only way students can learn anything is if they teach it to them. It is possible that some kids have already learned a few things before coming to you. Bloom's Taxonomy offers guidance on what to do in this situation.

We should simply look at our list of verbs and identify a skill that shows greater depth than the proficient level. Let's look at our example again. In our sample rubric, students had to apply their knowledge of four concepts. To show their ability to apply their skills, we might ask them to ride their bikes and measure their ability to demonstrate the four measurable objectives of balance, coordination, gross motor skills, and dexterity. In most classes, you'd have some students who could do this and some who could not when we decide to assess it. In the past, most of us would probably look at a kid who could ride his bike proficiently and ask him to teach other kids how to ride or tell the student to begin working on a new standard. Again, there's nothing wrong with that, but it is not necessarily helping that proficient child grow.

What if we took the verb *analyze* (a skill higher on the Bloom's Taxonomy pyramid) and asked our students to distinguish between the form and function of two bike designs? What if we had them *evaluate* professional BMX riders and determine who had a more advanced skill set? What if we had them *create* and *design* a new form of transportation that requires all four components of bike riding but in unique ways? Can you see how this could encourage our kids to become innovators and creators? Can you imagine the energy in your classroom as your students work tirelessly to demonstrate they are proficient in a standard so they can then begin to create and design? Who knew assessment could be such a motivating force for kids?

In schools all across the country, teachers are using this new approach to assessment to challenge the instruction they provide students. I've seen teachers turn a basic four-point rubric into an eight-point rubric using each of Bloom's levels plus a level for reflection. These teachers work with teachers at other grade levels and create a master rubric for their entire department. For example, a sixth-grade teacher may be responsible for the first four columns and be asked to get students at least to a level 3 of application. The seventh-grade teacher is then able to make their starting point level 3 because she knows at least 80 percent of her students are beginning there and she moves to columns 3, 4, 5, and 6 trying to get 80 percent of her students to synthesis. Then, the eighth-grade teacher jumps in and moves to the last four columns on their master rubric.

This level of complexity and coordination is taking this understanding to a remarkable level. I have seen some schools use these rubrics in every classroom and move away from grading individual assignments. In a gradebook, teachers begin assigning scores of one to four on each individual learning objective. Some schools hold onto letter grades to supposedly ease the transition for parents; they translate scores from one to four into letter grades. Ultimately, how these rubrics are translated into student labels is not important; what really matters is how teachers can use this information to enhance the teaching they do. These rubrics can be used to assess students using an unlimited number of tasks because it's not the task that is important. We aren't trying to determine a student's level of compliance in completing work; we're trying to determine what a child knows so we can give him or her more knowledge.

If you begin creating your rubrics and you have a singular project or activity in mind, stop right there. If this is done correctly, a single rubric can be used by all teachers responsible for the same standard regardless of the projects, tasks, or pedagogical styles used. As long as teachers are willing to talk and debate openly about what evidence is satisfactory to demonstrate understanding, there are no limits. At the end of a school year, a teacher may end up with a dozen rubrics, one for each standard that the teacher uses to assess all students all year long.

As a teacher, you are susceptible to bias and misinterpretation from time to time. Although you are the most important tool available to your students, you must check for validity. When state assessment scores become public, your scores should be showing student growth consistent with what you saw in your classroom. Your students are showing a mastery of standards that should translate into the ability to show understanding in a variety of formats, even a standardized test. I have seen evidence of this in every district and school that has adopted this method.

The following year, teachers at the next grade level should see evidence that your students have retained the knowledge you promised. If not, as a teacher with bold humility, you must be willing to reflect on what you have created. Do you need to realign the order in which you are teaching specific standards to better match up with other subjects or classes? Maybe you need to reevaluate the standards you found as the most powerful. You need to harness and evaluate your power as a teacher just as you need to assess your students' progress.

As the months and years pass, your expertise in the use of rubrics will evolve and grow as well and show a greater understanding. Perhaps you started with ten distinct rubrics measuring ten unique power standards, and now you have one large master rubric with fifty embedded skills. Maybe now you are cutting and pasting skills across standards to have units of study that allow you to assess skills from a number of standards all in one unit. Perhaps you are embracing the work of Rick Womeli and allowing students multiple retries to demonstrate proficiency and not just relying on one attempt. Maybe you are throwing caution to the wind and embracing the work of Dave Burgess and teaching like a pirate to get your students excited about learning content that you know to be essential to their development.

Using a rubric of learning derived from a power standard helps with standards-based grading and allows a practitioner of knowledge, a scientist, a teacher to become an artist. It allows a teacher to look at a canvas and evolve it based on its specific needs and abilities. It turns assessment into a diagnostic instrument, not a label-making machine.

Learning comes in so many forms and fashions. Reading helps many people grow, but it's not for everyone. A paper-and-pencil test helps us label achievement but does little to help us shape our instruction. My mission as a teacher is to help kids achieve greater levels of competence and understanding. My job is to change destinies. My job is to create students who may not be perfect today but will be successful tomorrow. My job is to capture a child's curiosity, fan its flames, and use it to my advantage. I will do all this by teaching to the test—the test of life. I will use every resource available because it's not about the process, it's about the progress. I want to be bold enough to stand up for what is best for my kids and humble enough to realize that my way is not the only way and to cheer my kids on every step of the way.

Chapter 6

Step 6: Make Practice Fun

Once children learn to ride bikes, they'll want to ride constantly, and it won't matter to them where they go; they just want to have fun. One thing they'll never ask to do is to complete a worksheet to prove they can ride bikes. They will never ask if they can ride independently for twenty minutes to build stamina or ride twenty laps to increase endurance. They want to just have fun and make their new skill a part of who they are by playing and finding their own ways to incorporate it into their day to day. Practice should be fun if we want it to be sustained. It should be child driven, encouraged, and frequent. Most important in all this, though, is that it should lead to continued growth.

As a former middle-school social studies teacher, I had a rule for my students. On Mondays, I'd let them know what we would be learning that week. If I couldn't clearly articulate how that learning would help them in life, students had the right to veto my ideas. This challenged me to determine the relevance of all I did. I often fell short, however, on this concept. I would often spend hours planning for my powerfully engaging lesson that would wow the kids and hook them in during my fifty-minute period. Then, once the kids left my room, everything stopped; I didn't provide any opportunities for continued, relevant practice. Sure, I would send kids home with some homework to do (a practice I am now actually opposed to), but what I often sent them home with was far less engaging than what I had them do with me. My own arrogance often got in the way. I would think that real learning could happen only while a child was with me, but in reality, most learning actually happens during the reflections after any one experience.

As an adult learner, I often have a difficult time falling asleep at night because of all that is in my head from the day. My children are notorious for calling me back into their rooms after I have tucked them in because they are thinking about something that occurred previously and they are now making some connection.

When my kids first began riding bikes, they learned the basics from me, but their ability to skid to a stop, jump curbs, and really become masters of the skill often happened when I was nowhere around. It happened because they wanted to practice and play. They wanted to get better. When I had my own classroom, I fell into the trap of believing that all learning was dependent on me. Just as my kids would have lost a passion for riding if I gave them a checklist of tasks to complete during scripted riding practice time, my students often lost interest at home because what was engaging in class was turned into a task at home. Students spent fifty minutes learning from me, but instead of fanning those flames when sending them off, I often smothered the flames by making them jump through worthless hoops.

Practice has to be fun. Make it collaborative with friends. Make it driven by student choice. Make it whatever the kids want as long as they are trying something new with the foundational skills you helped them acquire.

Some of my best friends are literacy experts who teach reading to children ages five to fifteen. They believe in what they are doing and are very good at it. The students they work with are typically identified through a variety of assessments as being in need of special interventions. Teachers across America are asked to give these assessments with increasing frequency to identify those struggling with basic literacy. This type of work is extremely valuable and needed. My issue is not with those giving children the skills to read but with the system's seemingly singular emphasis on this lone skill.

As a father of four, I spend approximately two hours every night reading to my kids. Each child gets alone time with me before bed; we say our prayers and read a few books together. This is my favorite time of each day. It is an opportunity for me to sit down one on one with my children individually, captivate their imaginations, and teach them something they may not have had the chance to learn on their own. My three youngest children (a baby, a three-year-old, and a five-year-old at the time of this writing) love picture books. Dr. Seuss, H. A. Rey, and William Steig are staples with their stories of mischief and make-believe. My kids love to look at the colorful illustrations as I read aloud the nonsensical stories and smile while interpreting the text.

My eleven-year-old enjoys a good story at night as well. He and I, however, do not share picture books anymore. Now it is more *Magic Tree House*, *I Survived*, or a good James Patterson. My son will tuck himself into bed, close his eyes, and just listen as I spin the tale described for us on the page. He will often fall asleep before I finish reading more than a few pages and probably drift into a dream about whatever plot was being described.

So how can a man who gets to experience such a time as this every night, a time of uninterrupted solitude with just his children and a good book, claim to believe that reading is overrated? I don't claim that at all. I love to read. I love sharing these moments with them and reading to them. During these moments, my kids oftentimes have their eyes closed and are making mental images without looking at a single printed word. They find themselves lost in the stories as they listen to my words, but they don't have to decode anything as they'd have to do if they were reading alone. I am basically playing the role of a storyteller, stealing a few minutes of alone time with each of them, and they love it.

In my career, I have traveled quite a bit around my region and across the country. I love listening to audio books when I fly. In the car, I listen to the radio—ESPN or perhaps a game, or talk radio (politics and religion mostly). I love learning about the world or getting a mental image of a baseball, basketball, or football game thousands of others are watching in person or on TV. Simply hearing someone else's description of the game allows my imagination to soar. Reading the score in the next day's paper just isn't the same as hearing it live, seeing it on TV (if I can get the remote away from my kids), or the ultimate experience, being in a stadium and experiencing the sights, sounds, smells, and adrenaline rush of being in the moment. Reading about an event is better than nothing, but experiencing it live is so much more exhilarating.

As a public-school principal, I see evidence of this every year when teachers try to sell me on a field trip plan. I always ask them to run their ideas by me so we can evaluate any one trip's learning potential. Inevitably, each teacher begins his or her pitch with something like, "I want them to see what we've been learning about in person." That's all I need to hear for me to say "Yes!" "I want them to see what we've been learning"—that statement lets me know these teachers understand what learning is all about. You can gain some knowledge, awareness, and learning through the printed word, but lasting learning comes from experiences. It's one thing to learn about animal habitats by reading a science textbook, but going to a zoo makes that learning come alive.

There's a reason so many parents go into debt each summer to take vacations—reading about the Grand Canyon is nothing like standing on its rim. Living a vacation is a lot more memorable than reading about one. As teachers, we are all about making memories; that's what learning is all about.

At this point, some of you may be relishing the irony of my

claiming—in writing—that reading is not as important a skill as it used to be. But let me stress again that I'm not opposed to reading because it's a great strategy, a great process geared toward a goal—learning—but it's not the only strategy or process that can help students learn. I'm well aware of the irony of putting such thoughts into print, but I know what happens when a book or article comes out—the author begins sharing and speaking about it even more. This book may not be something every educator picks up and flips through to gain insights, but it may be something a few people read, and I hope they will share their thoughts with others and start a dialogue in the process.

I received a doctorate in 2011. Part of that process involved writing a dissertation. What I wrote about is not as important for this analogy as is the process I went through. Even after writing what amounted to a book, after sharing countless drafts with college professors, after giving it to a professional editor to format and many colleagues to critique, my degree was not conferred upon me until I presented my findings to my dissertation committee and answered their countless questions in person. I had a written text that everyone in the room had read, but it was the presentation that helped shed light on the topic.

For those of you in education, think about the likes of Dave Burgess, Rick Womeli, or Robert Marzano. They have each written amazing books that have helped shape the educational landscape, but their presentations at speaking engagements are what pack meeting rooms and really inspire and change career destinies. Their writings are great in that they allow people across the world to gain exposure to their thoughts, but ultimately, their writings open the doors for real learning that occurs usually when they're in the room with you.

Let me explain this with another example. Before I became a school administrator, I was a middle-school teacher. I taught social studies and language arts to puberty-stricken youngsters. As a part of my social studies curriculum, I was asked to teach a bunch of thirteen-year-olds about a bunch of dead people from 2,000 years ago in ancient Greece and Rome and get them to understand why any of that was important to their lives in the twenty-first century. Lucky for me, I was given a great textbook to assist me. The book had vocabulary words in bold print, comprehension questions at the end of every chapter, and an index to help the kids find key information.

For those of you who are new to the world of teaching, no matter what subject you teach, nothing will ruin the thrill of learning for young kids as much as telling them to grab their textbooks, copy vocabulary words, and answer guided questions at the end of a chapter. When teaching about the Greeks, feel free to create a class Olympics. When teaching about Troy, have your students develop a Trojan horse to trick the class next door. Feel free to create a class hieroglyphic code and encourage students to pass notes when studying the Egyptians. Reading a textbook is one way to teach the information, but having kids create experiences is a much better way to have students learn the information. The textbook may offer clarity or light a spark of curiosity, but lasting learning occurs often in other ways.

In my language arts class, I was asked to teach the basics of poetry. One of the points I always made to my students was that great poetry was to be heard, not just read. In our classes, we had regular poetry slams. We discussed the power of music and how it captures our souls through rhythm and rhyme as the written word may not be able to. As a huge fan of music, I have told the thousands of students I have taught about my obsession with Tim McGraw and his music. Tim, like most country music stars, doesn't write the majority of his songs; Nashville is filled with professional songwriters who write the lyrics and have their words purchased by the artists who get to sing and perform and garner most of the credit and praise.

I've been a Tim McGraw fan for going on twenty years. I own all his CDs and have them downloaded on my phone as well. Tim has been blessed to have had dozens of number-one hits and is played on country radio nationwide. In the past twenty years, one thing I haven't done is buy any CDs put out by any of his songwriters who often dabble in becoming performers themselves. Nor have I gone to see any of the songwriters in concert. They are all extremely gifted at what they do; Tim McGraw would not be nearly as successful without them, but he is the one I am a fan of, not them.

I listen to his music constantly in my office, and anytime he comes to town, I'm the first to buy a ticket to his concert. His music and performance draw me in so much more than the lyrics to his songs. The words to the songs are often deep, but it is the musical interpretation of them that gives the words lasting value for me. I could just sit back and read the lyrics, but I guarantee you it would not have the same effect as hearing them.

I want to make a few things clear before we jump into some more educational jargon. First, I want to state again that I love to read. I love curling up with a good book, learning about the world, or exploring a great narrative with dramatic plot twists. I also understand that not everyone enjoys the quiet solitude required for this type of activity. While I may enjoy reading *To Kill a Mockingbird*, others may enjoy going on Netflix and watching Gregory Peck play the role of Atticus Finch. Although I may prefer to watch SportsCenter to get my daily sporting update, others may prefer the morning paper. In no way do I want people to think I'm not a supporter of teaching students to read or that I don't believe reading is a valuable skill. I do believe it is valuable and can serve as one of the key methods for acquiring knowledge. I also believe, however, that there are countless other ways to gain understanding. I'm a proponent of making learning fun, dynamic, and personal. If we want our kids to take their learning with them and practice it in ways that allow them to grow, we have to understand that not all students learn the same way we do but that's perfectly okay.

I also believe our students need to do more than just learn how to gain information; they must learn how to analyze, synthesize, and evaluate it as well. Just because you read it doesn't make it true. Just because you know it doesn't mean you can use it. Our kids need to understand this. We need to take their learning to new heights. We need to make it real and relevant.

This week when you are trying to figure out how to help your children practice, here are a few helpful hints.

- Don't make them go home and read more about the topic.
- Don't make every child do the same thing—worksheets are passion killers.
- If you can't think of ideas, ask your students for some.
- If your students can't think of ways, examine your lesson. Maybe it wasn't as dynamic and transformational as you thought.

Chapter 7

Step 7: Let Them Go and Let Them Grow

This takes us to the seventh and final piece of the bike-riding metaphor. It's okay if they get better than you. Really, it is. You will never see me jumping curbs, riding no-handed, or asking my friends to jump on my pegs to go for a tandem ride on my ten-speed mountain bike. I'm not sure I could do those things. You know who can, though? My kids, who are all at least thirty years younger than me.

Nowadays, kids are exposed to stunt riders and trick riders all over the Internet. They see these amazing athletes doing tricks I have never even imagined, and they want to duplicate them. Me, I'm okay going for a nice Sunday afternoon ride to buy a coffee and a donut, but that's not good enough for them. My kids want to find some trails and some hills to jump. They want to push their limits.

As a middle-aged man in America, I have my own comfort zone and a preferred way of bike riding just as I have a preferred method of learning. I love to read, and I love to take leisurely rides just as much. My kids, not so much. As a dad, I can sit my children down and tell them they need to do things the same way as I do, or I can tell them the sky's the limit and they are free to pass me by. It's okay if I'm not comfortable with what they're doing. It's okay if I sit on the sidelines and watch them do jumps and tricks that I never attempt as long as I don't in turn try to squash their enthusiasm for being better than me.

As a parent with four kids of various ages, I understand what it means to have children at a wide range of ability and cognitive levels. What I don't understand is why we as adults try to classify ability levels into neat little boxes as much as we do. For example, my eleven-year-old son is a great bike rider. He hops on, jumps curbs, pops wheelies, and sometimes is caught going no-handed in spite of my cautions for him to stay safe. I'm a bike rider as well. Sometimes, I can be found riding my mountain bike pulling a toddler trailer. I do not do jumps or ride no-handed. If someone were to evaluate my skills as a bike rider, I would clearly be deemed proficient. I don't fall down or crash into cars or pedestrians. My eleven-year-old son, however, definitely has more skills than I do or is at least a bigger risk taker. If the two of us were to put on an exhibition for evaluators with my son going first, would they classify him as riding at an eleven-year-old level? Would this mean he is performing at a level comparable to his peers? What about me? I'm three decades older. Should my goal be to be identified as riding at an eleven-year-old level or at a cautious yet proficient forty-year-old level? What would the requirements be to be identified as proficient? Would they be based on balance, risk taking, speed, ability to shift gears, apply the brakes, and so on? What is the most important feature? As a cautious rider, I would argue that safety is the most important element, but my son would argue risk taking. A professional rider may argue speed or endurance.

In schools, we constantly place labels on kids based on our subjective opinions of what they should be able to do. A child may be a third grader with ADHD reading at a first-grade level, but what does any of this mean, and what do we do about it?

In my school, in my classrooms, just as in my house, I'm okay if my kids don't want to read. I want them to learn. I want them to grow. I want them to do more than I ever imagined possible. I want to help them do it by guiding them, supporting them, and helping them appreciate that we are all different and that's okay. I love my kids. I love my job. I love to learn, and I want them all to know that whether they read it, hear it, or feel it. Knowing it is all that matters.

As I am writing this, my kids are all home on spring break. My oldest, in fifth grade, has spent the last year and a half adjusting to the way school works in Florida. Last summer, we moved to Florida from Michigan, and I can state emphatically that schools in these two states are not the same. At his previous school, he was assessed three times a year on his reading ability and was always told he was reading above grade level, whatever that meant.

The concept of being at grade level reminds me of the charts I get from the pediatrician letting me know that my children are all in the 90th percentile for weight and height. Does this mean I should worry that they will all grow to be giants and tower above all but 10 percent of their friends and family, or should I just be concerned if they are an outlier in the other direction? Should these statistics cause alarm only if the majority of others are seemingly better off? Does having a son who reads above his grade level mean he is smarter than his peers? Does it mean he can learn more than his peers can? If it were that simple, he probably wouldn't need to bring home a report card outlining his performance in every subject area. After all, reading is all that matters, and if he can read, he will know more than those who can't, right?

Well, here in Florida, he receives a report card every nine weeks that provides him with an aggregate grade for each core subject area. Last week, he brought home a report card that showed a grade of C+ in science, B- in social studies, A- in math, and an A in reading. His lowest grade was in science, but he spends approximately eight hours a week watching the Science Channel on TV. He will bypass Nickelodeon and the Disney Channel to get to *Myth Busters* or *How It's Made*. As a result, he can explain how just about any common household object is made. He can explain how the universe is expanding, how planes can fly, and how El Niño affects weather patterns across North America, yet he has his lowest grades in a subject he has the most interest and arguably the most knowledge in. How is that possible?

I have a son who can pass a reading test and demonstrate an understanding of complex phenomena, but he's assessed to be at a level that is less than prolific. A while back, I had a conversation with one of his teachers that I later transcribed.

Me: "Mrs. F, I am hoping you can explain some of Cameron's grades to me."

Mrs. F: "Well, sure. He is a smart kid. If he would just work harder his grades would improve."

Me: "Thank you for saying that. I hope I don't come across rudely here, but how do you know he is smart?"

Mrs. F: "Well he knows so much. He participates in all our conversations and is always challenging the status quo."

Me: "That's great, but I am confused. Can you explain his grades?"

Mrs. F: "Sure. Our tests and assignments are all based off of things we read in class. If he doesn't read, he won't do well. I have told him he needs to just read for about twenty minutes each night and he will do so much better."

Me: "Oh. Thanks, however, he doesn't learn through reading. He reads for fun. He spends his mornings watching the Science Channel and his afternoons with his brothers and sister or outside playing baseball with his peers. Which of these activities do you think he should give up so that he can start reading more?"

Mrs. F: "Well that's not for me to say, but if he doesn't start doing things the way everyone else does, his grades will stay the same."

Me: "I am so sorry. I didn't realize everyone else in the class had an A in every subject. I will adjust my son's schedule today."

Mrs. F: "Not every student has an A, but the good ones do."

Me: "I get it. My son is not one of the good ones. I have one request. Feel free to tell me I am crazy, but is it possible that you are defining 'the good kids' by looking for the kids who learn things the same way you do? Is it possible that some kids learn things in different ways and can then demonstrate their understanding in different ways? If so, as a teacher, is it possible that some kids will learn the same way you do and some will not and that it is your job to figure out how to reach every child?"

Mrs. F: "I have a class with more than twenty students. I cannot possibly figure out the unique ways every child learns. Sometimes, I have to look for the ways that will reach the most kids and hope everyone can just follow along."

Me: "I completely get it. Reading is a great way to communicate ideas to the masses. It is easy to send all kids home with a book and ask them to read so they can all learn the same information. I do get it. I just hope that my child can learn from a teacher who is willing to do whatever is necessary to move his learning forward, not just doing what is convenient and easiest."

Right now, I'm sure many of you who are teachers are thinking one of two things: *Thank God his kids aren't in my class* or *Thank God I don't work in this guy's school.* I know I can be intense. In my own school, I have often said the greatest gift I can give my teachers is the ability to defend their craft. If they can't explain why they're doing what they're doing, they should stop immediately. We don't allow kids to shrug responsibility for their actions by saying they don't know why they do what they do. We should have at least that much of an expectation of our teachers. Teachers need to be willing to go beyond what is convenient and be able to argue for what is best. To argue for what's best, they must know what's best. They must be able to sit back at the end of the day and determine whether it was a good or bad day at work. They should know whether their students learned. If learning is dependent on reading, teachers could in theory just spend their planning time figuring out what textbook pages to assign. If kids show up having read what was assigned, they'll learn, right? It's all about the textbooks, right? Of course not. Teachers teach.

To teach, a teacher must identify what kids know, what they need to know, and how they will learn it. We have to get beyond telling students they simply need to try harder, study more, read more, and do what we do to learn and be successful. As the adults, we must be willing to adjust our notions of what learning looks like and meet students where they are to move them forward. It seems like a daunting task, but rest assured, it's not as complex as you might think. Let me walk you through a few more metaphors to guide you through how this works for you.

I get up at 4:30 a.m. each day. I start my mornings with a jog and get in twenty-five to thirty miles a week. I spend three or four evenings a week lifting weights. I don't eat dessert, and have at least five servings of fruit and vegetables each day. I'm forty, and I weigh 167 pounds. I ask you now, am I healthy? Based on what you know, can you draw a conclusion? I'm assuming most of you would say, "yes".

But what if I told you that my dad's dad passed away at age forty-two from a heart attack and that my dad had his first heart attack five years ago at age fifty-five? What if I told you that on my mom's side, cancer and depression were common and that my grandmother passed away while experiencing dementia? Does this information change your analysis of my health? How much information do you need before you can label me healthy or unhealthy? Is my health assessment relative to yours and others? Do your own experiences and history affect your ability to analyze me?

The last time you went to the doctor for a checkup, what tests did the doctor run to determine your health? Quite possibly, your height, weight, blood pressure, sight, and hearing were all measured. Perhaps some blood work was ordered and maybe even a few scans were done. Your doctor recognizes that health is a complex determination. Your body is made up of numerous systems that all have an impact on your overall health. Your doctor could assess every system in your body every day if you wanted, but time and money often restrict us from such intrusive measures.

Instead, your doctor may look at your history, run some simple tests, and determine how best to follow up. Maybe he will order more labs, or maybe he'll give you a clean bill of health. Regardless of the result, your doctor will often take your results and refer you to a specialist or offer some simple suggestions on how to improve your results next time and then ask you to come back at a future date so he can measure your progress. Rarely will a doctor simply state, "You're healthy" or "You're unhealthy." He'll typically compare your results to some norms and let you know how you compare. He won't just run tests and not let you know the results. We expect immediate feedback and guidance. Heath, like learning, is not binary; it's something that can be compared to a standard, assessed relative to others, and monitored over time. We would expect nothing less from our medical professionals.

As educators, we must embrace the same mind-set in our classrooms. We cannot label students as special ed (and therefore incapable of showing success), gifted (and capable of more than others), at grade level, below grade level, C students, problem students, at-risk students, and so on. Though such labels are convenient for compartmentalizing students, they're often counterproductive in helping us actually do our job, which is helping each individual child grow in his or her understanding of very specific learning targets and to reach his or her maximum potential, not our predetermined limits.

Just as learning can come in a variety of ways, so too does our ability to assess it. Taking a multivitamin in the morning helps me stay healthy, but as I have recently learned, if my eating habits are well rounded, a pill once a day to gain vitamins and minerals isn't needed. It's one way to gain what I need, but not the only way. In our classrooms, our job is to create healthy learners capable of getting healthier through a variety of methods. We cannot force one diet on all and expect every child to gain the same results.

Walk into your local GNC store and ask a sales rep for the one diet or nutritional supplement that works for everyone and you will hear that there is no such miracle drug. We have to understand the same is true in our classrooms. Reading is one way to gain knowledge and information, but so is watching a movie, debating, listening to a lecture, conducting a lab, playing a game, and so on.

Taking my weight and blood pressure are important for a doctor to gather baseline information, but that's far from a complete assessment of my health. A test in class this Friday assessing content knowledge or students' reading levels may be a good way to gain a limited scope of their levels of understanding, but it doesn't paint a complete picture of knowledge or how to help it progress. In some ways, this limits us as we have measured only one strategy for learning and have used this singular measurement to cast broad labels over all future learning potential.

Our kids need guidance. We need to assess their abilities. Our assessments and our guidance, however, should never be used to determine where a kid may go. They are useful only to determine where they are. We need to believe that when we get out of the way, kids will actually grow more than if we put them in a box we've designated just for them.

Chapter 8

My Own Experience

In sixth grade, my social studies class learned about World War II, and I was fascinated by what I learned. I grew up in a military household with a father actively serving in the navy, one grandfather having served in the Korean Conflict, and another grandfather having served in the Pacific Theater during the conclusion of the war with Germany and Japan.

As a twelve-year-old, I was hungry for knowledge on the subject of the world wars so I could better relate to the experiences of the men in my life. In class, I devoured our social studies textbook and made multiple trips to our school media center to check out additional books on the subject.

One evening, I read a book with pictures of the Holocaust and the German concentration camps. I asked my dad about the Japanese internments camps we had here in America, something I'd never heard about. My dad told me that America had had its own camps to house citizens we considered threats. *Why didn't I read about this in any of the books in my school library?* I wondered.

I talked with my school librarian and learned that our school purchased books that allowed for students to be filled only with hope and pride. Books that described some of our country's less-than-spectacular moments didn't fit that mold. Even today, many school libraries have banned certain books; they censor the information they make available to kids. Some municipalities have done similar things with adult-oriented texts as well.

In some places, individuals do not use books to help spread a wide range of knowledge but to ingrain specific beliefs. Some would argue, "This just proves that we need our kids to be well read, to have exposure to a lot of texts, and to gain a lot more knowledge." I don't disagree, but I think if we center our conversation on simply teaching students how to receive information through decoding the written text, we're missing the point and doing them a disservice. If getting kids to read what's put before them is all we're after, our kids will miss out on a lot of knowledge and lose the ability to start forming their own opinions. We do not just want our children to learn about the past; we want our children to make our futures better.

Reagan, my five-year-old, loves princesses, queens, and Barbies. Her room is pink, and her closet is filled with dresses. She is the sweetest little lady. Last summer, I read her a book at night that I had loved when I was a kid. It was a Sesame Street–themed book with Grover, that fluffy blue Muppet, describing that there was a monster at the end of the book. Throughout the book, Grover implores readers to stop reading so they do not get any closer to the end of the book because of his fear of monsters. Lo and behold, on the last page, the readers learn that the monster at the end of the book is only Grover—there was nothing to be afraid of.

The book is cute and has just enough suspense to hold the attention of a four-year-old. What I didn't account for was the nightmare it would provoke in her. At that stage in her mental development, my little girl had not come to understand the elements of fiction. She didn't know she was supposed to analyze the text and pictures to deduce that the story wasn't real. She had a hard time distinguishing between fact and fiction. She took the text at face value, believing it to be 100 percent true, and fell asleep with monsters on her mind.

Far too often, our students, and many of us for that matter, fall into the same trap. We have a simple comprehension of the text but haven't developed more-complex skills such as analysis, synthesis, and evaluation that would allow us to draw our own conclusions. Look at any political advertisement in America today and you will see firsthand that this is exactly what many politicians depend on. Many people who read the written word simply take it at face value and run with it without a second thought of analyzing it for accuracy.

In 1956, child psychologist Dr. Benjamin Bloom shared his vision for education in which he promoted the need for more high-order thinking. Developed during the first decade of the Cold War, this taxonomy of thinking equipped educators with a tool that they could use to better focus their energies on skills of greater depth. In an era focused on the space race, nuclear ambitions, and computer innovation, developing students with the ability to acquire knowledge and then do something with it was of paramount importance.

According to Bloom and his team, the progression of cognitive learning follows the pattern shown below.

1. knowledge
2. comprehension
3. application
4. analysis
5. synthesis
6. evaluation

In 2000, this taxonomy was revised to allow for a change in syntax from nouns to verbs, but the basic premise remained the same.

When I was in school thirty years ago, my teachers focused on ensuring the acquisition of knowledge. I had weekly spelling tests and was asked to recite my multiplication facts. I was asked to memorize the presidents and the capitals of each state. My teachers wanted to make sure that my mind was filled with enough information that I could win any game of Trivial Pursuit I played; I was set up to be a *Jeopardy* champion even if I never auditioned for the show.

When I was in middle school, my parents bought a set of encyclopedias. They saw that my mind was absorbing a lot of information at school but that I was hungry for more. I would come home from school and tell my parents that Richmond was the capital of Virginia but would ask why that was the case since it wasn't the state's largest city. I would look at a map of the United States and ask why western states covered so much more geographical area than those on the East Coast. I wanted to know why the sky was blue but space was black. Why was the grass green when the dirt was brown? I would question everything.

As a result of my constant questioning, my parents bought that set of encyclopedias. I'm still not sure if that was an attempt to shut me up or help me learn, but these books contained the answers to almost any question I could ask; they were the text equivalent of Google. If I could look up a key word alphabetically, I could find information galore. In those books, I learned the history of the Civil War in fewer than five pages. I learned who Henry Ford was, how far the earth was from the sun, the history of the Cold War, and countless other facts. Those books gave me greater understanding of the world at least as it existed in the 1980s through the lens of the editors of the book.

Thirty years ago, gaining knowledge, greater understanding, and comprehension was a sign of intelligence. As a matter of fact, my ability to recall so many facts earned me a spot in the gifted and talented program at my school even though my dad often said to me that I had book smarts but no common sense. I was even told once, "You may get all A's in school, but in the real world, A students end up working for the C students."

At the time, I was highly offended, but today, I think that statement has some validity. My quest for knowledge was limiting my ability to search for more-complex learning. I was filled with useless facts. While others were outside playing and living life, I was in my room reading about life.

Fast-forward thirty years—I heard on the radio this week that a large city here in America was proposing legislation that would require restaurants to place a picture of a saltshaker next to menu items that contained more than the recommended daily intake of sodium. A reporter stated that this would be placed on children's and adults' menus alike. When my family goes out to eat, it's often my job to order for my children. Sometimes, we're lucky enough to go to restaurants where there are pictures of the food choices allowing some of my kids to advocate for themselves. If they see pictures of pizza, macaroni and cheese, or chicken fingers, I know I'll have some happy kids.

Once when I was at a national restaurant chain, next to the pictures of menu items was an indication of the number of calories in each serving. The caloric information meant nothing to three of my kids, but my eleven-year-old wanted to know what a calorie was. I explained that it was basically the energy available in this or that item that could get turned into fat if not used up, and I could tell he had some basic understanding of the concept. He took that knowledge and was able to apply it to the food choice he was considering (but still went with a slice of pepperoni pizza).

I am not naïve enough to believe that the restaurant put the calorie information on the menu for the benefit of kids making their dietary decisions; it was there for their parents. We were to make decisions based on that information. I assume this is the logic behind the saltshaker pictures as well and warning labels on packs of cigarettes.

The overwhelming majority of Americans understand that too much sodium, too many calories, and smoking are bad for healthy lifestyles, but our inability to analyze that information and to make wise decisions is our downfall. Gaining the ability to analyze, synthesize, evaluate, create, and reflect is the primary purpose for acquiring information, yet these are the skills we often glance right over in schools today. We focus so intently on getting our students to memorize and recall information that we never move to anything deeper. We're content if our kids can read labels on cans or boxes of food; we rarely go the extra step of teaching them how to make informed decisions along with their newfound knowledge.

That's the heart of my argument in this text. I don't care how my children acquire understanding whether from a written text, digital media, pictures on a menu, or their friends and family. I want them to do something with the information they take in.

The skill of analysis is basically what I am doing with this book; I'm attempting to break a large concept down into its components. I did not just throw out the statement "I don't care if my kids choose to read"; I'm explaining why I think that and what that statement means beyond a surface-level understanding by dissecting my feelings, the research, and what it means to read and think. The skill of analysis is what makes good teachers great and great coaches winners.

Over the last two decades, sports radio has become a major player in the media world; it's moved beyond providing updates once an hour or simply reporting game scores. There are now stations that devote twenty-four hours a day to breaking down the last game won or lost by your hometown heroes into its subtleties. These stations have listeners clogging up the phone lines eager to offer their assessments of why the home team won or lost. Great coaches do this same thing in their offices daily as they determine practice and improvement plans. Breaking abstract concepts down into smaller chunks is the starting point. Coming up with a game plan based on those subtleties is the art of synthesizing. These are two complex skills that when done well will often turn a coach into a winning coach.

I have coached a few sports in my time at the youth and high school levels. I have spent time on the volleyball and basketball courts, running track, and even helping guide golfers around a course. Each game came with its own expectations, outcomes, and rules, and as the coach, it was my job to use all these nuances to get the most out of my athletes. Back in 2007, I coached a basketball team that went undefeated. The team had tremendous amounts of talent, but more important than that, its members played as a team.

When the team was initially constructed, I first looked at each player individually. I knew that I wanted players who could shoot, dribble, pass, rebound, defend, and move, the key components of well-developed players. An analysis of the game helped me make that determination. As I examined my players, I began to rank each one to determine their relative strengths with each component. Based upon their scores on my rubric, players were then placed in primary positions. Some became guards, others became forwards, and a couple played center. I took "basketball player" as a concept that I had an understanding of, analyzed the key features, and synthesized that information by creating groupings and themes based on the data collected. As the season went on, our practices were designed around those key components as we tried to maximize our strengths and minimize our weaknesses. I wanted to make sure that each practice had a theme designed to improve a specific skill.

I set aside time each week to watch film. Sometimes, I would bring in videos showing other teams. We would watch them work and then break down their strengths and weaknesses, determine what we would need to do to exploit them, and ultimately evaluate what they did well.

The more advanced skill of evaluation is basically making judgments based on facts and evidence. By breaking down what we saw on film, we were in essence coming up with our evidence to present our case. Inevitably, because I had a confident team, each film session ended with our players determined and believing that we were better than the team we watched and that we could beat everyone. But that belief, that evaluation, was never good enough.

For some reason, the officials always still made us play the game. They never let our players just come up to them before tip-off and state that the game should be cancelled because we already knew we were better. To be undefeated, they had to actually move beyond their evaluations and play the game.

As our season progressed, our games got tougher. In our league, each team played the other teams twice. During the first half of the season, our raw talent was often enough to defeat our opponents. Our players knew they had more skill, but so did the other coaches. When we entered the second half of the season, it became apparent that the other coaches had been studying us just as we had been studying them. They had identified some of our flaws and were doing all they could to take advantage of them. My job was to not only scout the other teams but also to convince our athletes that they needed to get better.

We spent countless hours watching film of our own games, games that we won, and games we thought we played well to figure out what we could do better. This level of reflection was difficult. Honest reflection is often difficult for most people, but it often allows learners to grow. My athletes were not simply given a test on the rules to determine their knowledge and comprehension of basketball. They were not asked to simply explain the attributes of successful players and then group them into similarities and differences. They were asked to take all their knowledge, to go out and create something great, and to keep working to make it better. This is what learning is really all about. It's not enough to just have knowledge; it's a matter of doing something with it, to make informed decisions, to keep growing, and to keep improving.

When I was a kid, I learned a lot about sports by picking up my encyclopedias, reading my baseball cards, or looking at *Sports Illustrated*. Today, kids have access to SportsCenter almost twenty-four hours a day, can play lifelike video games, and watch highlights on YouTube. They are accessing information in different ways, but ultimately, where they get it from doesn't matter as much as their ability to validate the data, determine its relevance, evaluate what they are seeing, and do something with it.

When I was twelve, I'd watch AAA baseball; the Tidewater Tides were a minor league affiliate of the New York Mets playing out of Norfolk, Virginia where I lived at the time. I wanted to grow up and be one of the players on the field. I checked out *The Complete Baseball Encyclopedia* from the library; it was filled with pictures, graphics, and thousands of words describing the history of the game, strategies for winning, and countless seemingly arbitrary baseball facts. I spent a weekend reading that book, and then the next month, I tried to copy every word. I didn't use a copy machine; I grabbed pencil and paper. For whatever reason, I thought copying the text would turn me into a better baseball player. Instead of practicing the game, I spent days reading and writing about it. Sure, I gained a lot of knowledge about Babe Ruth, the infield fly rule, and the designated hitter, but my baseball skills didn't improve in the least.

I wonder how often our students and children in schools are forced into the same trap. How many times do we ask students to get buried in a book to learn about an aspect of life that they could learn so much better if we just let them experience it?

In today's educational systems, we begin preparing our children from preschool to become college and career ready. I completely understand the intent; we want to build and scaffold our instruction so our children will grow in aptitude and have options as adults. We are careful to make sure school curricula are aligned vertically so what a child learns in elementary school allows for greater success in middle school and then high school and beyond. There's a problem with this approach though.

I currently work as a school administrator. In every school building and school district I have ever worked in, the teachers with the least amount of experience have been paid the least. There is an understanding that teachers require on-the-job experience to gain the skills necessary to be highly effective. Coming right out of a college program with a teaching degree isn't enough. Teachers are expected to learn as they go. We believe that as they teach and gain on-the-job training, they will get better at their jobs, and then we compensate them accordingly. Professional football players don't earn their largest contracts straight out of college either; there are rookie salary caps that limit how much an unproven football player can make. The NFL draft is seen as a crapshoot as analysts wrestle with whether the skills seen in a college player will translate to the world of professional football. It is often the second contract, four years into a career, when an athlete has had the chance to learn the job by doing the job, that yields the big money.

We put so much attention in our schools to prepare students to be successful in careers, and then the real world comes and those former students learn that to be successful in their careers, they must actually experience their careers. If the aim of making a career ready adult is really the goal of every school in America, it seems as though we as adults should accept the idea that on the job training is not a requirement. We have already given them what they need to be prepared to be successful, or maybe we should come to realize that schools are not really doing what we have set out to do. We hope to prepare our students to live and succeed in the world while at the same time doing all we can to insulate them from the actual world they'll be living in.

In our schools, if we want to prepare our kids for their future, we must engage them in their present. We must give them real-world experiences by letting them experience the real world. Reading about the world to prepare them for their future does only so much. If we want our kids to be successful later on, we must follow through on the greatest parenting advice I ever received: "Do not ever begin a sentence with, 'I can't wait until ...'" Our job is to provide students with rich, engaging, real-world experiences that foster their natural curiosities. Then we must explicitly teach them multiple strategies to make meaning of the new world around them and then give them opportunities to analyze, synthesize, create, evaluate, reflect, and grow.

Let our kids be kids. Kids learn. Kids take risks. Kids create. Don't force them to sit, read, and digest limited perspectives. If a kid chooses to read to gain knowledge, outstanding. That's what works for me as an adult. If children grab an iPad, turn on the TV, or engage in conversation to acquire knowledge, outstanding. Let them gather their facts and information however they need to. Our larger goal should be helping them develop the skills to make meaning of the information being collected and to interpret all the information they're absorbing. Educators should teach skills that can be used with a variety of content, not just to infuse content that students cannot do anything with.

Chapter 9

Engagement or Standards: Which Is It?

I've been blessed in my career to have done a number of things outside my classroom and office. I've given presentations to a variety of audiences sharing some of what I have learned about standards-based grading, assessment, and student engagement. Some of you may be reading the words in this book and thinking, *I've heard this before*. Great! That help proves my overall point. You didn't need this book to teach you anything. You were able to learn without reading. Maybe we talked at a conference recently. Maybe you sat in one of my audiences. Maybe I have worked side by side with you. I also understand that reading may allow you to revisit concepts again or to have the time to learn at your own pace. It also allows me to share my ideas or the ideas I have borrowed from others with an audience that may not have had the ability to hear them before.

Aside from my ability to speak before audiences, I do some work for the accreditation agency known as Advanc-Ed. With this responsibility, I've been able to work with some amazing educational leaders from around the world and visit incredible schools and classrooms across the country. The work Advanc-Ed does on these accreditation visits does not focus on identifying a school's or a district's successes and failures; we believe that's an internal process.

The role of an accreditation team is to evaluate a system's process for self-assessment and reflection. Does a school system have its own processes and procedures for examining what's working and what needs improvement? Does it have a way to determine how to grow and meet the needs of more students? In essence, is the system learning? It is not a question of pass/fail; it's a question of where the system is on its journey.

Systems are neither good nor bad because they're all at different levels of development. Because systems are complex entities, we cannot simply identify a system comprising multiple individuals with varying experiences and roles as simply satisfactory or unsatisfactory. I have been on many external reviews, as we call these visits, where the schools' staff members don't understand that this is what we are there to explore. We often get the red-carpet treatment. Many places see this as a final exam and do all they can to just let us see their best and brightest so they can earn a passing grade and get a nice write-up in the local paper. They prep for days and put their best foot forward so the team can see the results of all their hard work. As a team, though, we aren't all that concerned with the show we see; we're there to examine evidence of a process that was in place before our arrival and one that will hopefully continue after we leave.

We're all guilty of putting on dog-and-pony shows like that once in a while. A politician a few years ago described this as putting lipstick on a pig. We try to disguise our struggles or flaws rather than address them. We mask what's really going on. Have you ever experienced something like this in your classroom or school? If you are an administrator, do you ever see teachers putting forth tremendous effort to create an artificial show on observation day because they want you to see only the finished and polished product? They don't want you to see the man behind the curtain, just the magical wizard.

How about your students? Are they expected to study for tests and quizzes every Thursday night because Friday is test day? Come

Saturday, they can forget it all, but on the day of the big test, they better know it and show it. There's no push for endurance, no focus on the learning process, only a quest for short-term memory, a quick experience, and content regurgitation. What goes in must come out. The problem with this is if we are focusing only on producing results that are replicas of what we already know, we'll never progress. If that's all we put in, that's all we'll get out.

We have strict trademark and copyright laws in America for a reason. Sure, we want to limit copycats for the sake of financial gain, but the laws go beyond trying to protect financial interests. By limiting replication in commercial and intellectual enterprises, we are also forcing innovation and creativity. When a law forbids others from simply stealing an idea, we're prompted to create something better. We cannot just accept what is and make it ours; we must take what is and make something new and better out of it. Similarly, some of you may decide to copy some of the ideas in this book, but what I really want is for you to try and discredit these ideas or perhaps enhance them to find a better way to do things. When we can't copy, we must create.

As teachers and educators, we will have a very difficult time getting our students to do something that we aren't comfortable doing. Creating is about risk taking. We have to create new realities and try things nobody else has tried. We need to create creators, risk takers, people willing to change their destinies. We need to create students not intimidated by failure and the true learning process. But how can we teach students to do something that we ourselves don't know how to do? How can we get kids to move beyond where we are able to take them? How do we create new thought? As teachers, we have spent our careers feeling comfortable being the smartest one in the room and encouraging our students to simply mimic what we already know. That way of teaching, however, simply isn't working. We teachers need to become facilitators of learning, not keepers of knowledge. We need to become feedback providers, not graders and labelers. We need to encourage our kids to take what we give them and make it better.

Standards-based grading and its cousin, standards-based learning, get a lot of attention from progressive educators today. Using the phrase coined by Stephen Covey, "Begin with the end in mind," we want to know where our students are going before we start them on their journey there. The standards are the goal—what we want to teach them, or more specifically what we want them to demonstrate evidence of having learned. How we get them there is the art of teaching. As educators, it's our responsibility to measure our students' progress toward their goals. It's our job to move each of them forward and closer to seeing success. At the heart of these movements is the idea that teachers must learn how to interpret standards and measure student work, commonly described as evidence, against a standard.

Some of you may have heard me make the seemingly redundant statement, "a standard is standard only if it is standard." I even made this statement earlier in this book. Whether I'm driving through Alabama or Michigan, I know that when I see a mile marker on the side of the road, I'll have to travel 5,280 feet before getting to the next marker. No matter where I am in the country, the standard for measuring a mile is the same; it doesn't change depending on the weather, the state, or the car I drive.

To help us have clarity in communication and expectation while driving, we must have a uniform method of interpreting a measurement. This keeps us safe, allows us to understand our limits, and helps us predict and plan for what will come. The standard is not up for interpretation, but we do have tremendous latitude in how we use that standard for our own benefit. The same is true with the standards presented to teachers.

Why is it, for example, that as we drive along interstates we see mile markers and not foot or meter markers? Because it would be an extraordinary expense and waste of resources, and we'd end up just littering the landscape with millions of such signs. Why do we have any signs at all to mark our progress? Why not just let all drivers figure out their own ways to chart progress? Some may want to use kilometers, others yards, and others speed. There is a reason we are all asked to use a standard measurement.

An inch is an inch on every ruler. When I was a kid, my goal was to grow up and be six foot three. (I worshiped Joe Dumars on the Detroit Pistons and according to my basketball cards, that was his height). I would measure myself often against a standard measurement looking at my progress. If I ever got to my ideal height (I'm just five ten today), I would not automatically stop growing just because that was my goal. I may continue to develop and grow and could still use my standard measurement to chart my progress. Being tall is not standard, nor is being short. Those descriptions are what statisticians would call norm-referenced or subjective interpretations; they're relative. Tall and short are descriptive words that require a comparison to another object. Based on our opinions or comparisons, we make judgments. Using an explicit standard, not a subjective comparison, I was able to determine if I was able to meet my goal.

A teacher may privately label one child as smart and another as slow based on the relative nature of the two students than on their abilities to understand or articulate an individual learning target. To a child, someone who is six feet may seem impressively tall, but in the NBA, that six-footer would be deemed short. In a standards-based classroom, the goal is to have a constant measurement as free from personal bias as possible. This does not necessarily mean we are looking to eliminate teacher autonomy, creativity, or individualism; in fact, it's the opposite. The goal is to create objective measurements of learning, not of teaching. A standards-based classroom actually enhances a teacher's ability to be creative and free. The standard is the "what" while the creativity of teaching is the "how".

What we test is what we teach. What we teach is what we value.

Have you ever tried to question other teachers on their grading scales, grade weighting, or classroom rules? Have you ever tried to debate some of the concepts presented earlier in this book like relative due dates and retakes and felt the tension in the room increase? I equate talking about grading and class norms with a teacher to talking politics and religion at Thanksgiving dinner with extended family. When you bring up certain topics even in the most innocent and exploratory manner, you can be seen as questioning a person's values and priorities. This puts others on defense feeling that their core is being challenged.

Reread the first two sentences of the last paragraph. If you test it, you value it. Sure, we can argue that our students are over-tested. We can say states and districts require us to test our students on things that we see little value in. Yet for some reason, we continue to do it. Many consider this something not worth fighting over anymore. Rebelling against the onslaught of testing could be career suicide. I am in no way advocating for that. In fact, I see tremendous value in testing, but we'll explore that later. What I'm saying here is simply that a test displays value. If a state or district mandates a test, it's saying the subject areas being tested are valuable even if you personally disagree. If you as a teacher give up class time to test your students, you're implying that there's a value to specific content or skills. You're sacrificing time that could have been spent doing any other number of activities when you stop to administer tests.

The problem is not that we are testing our students so much; the problem is that we don't all explicitly see the value that we are implying by doing so. We test our students religiously on Fridays, at the end of semesters, prior to entrance to kindergarten, seemingly in every classroom every day. We do this because someone somewhere has determined that testing students is important.

As teachers, we often play along with the testing game, and at the core, I have no problem with that. As a matter of fact, I think that in many classes we don't test enough. What? Did I just put that in print? So far in this book, I've said, "I don't care if my kids choose to read" and now I'm saying "We need to test more often"?

Before you put this book down and rattle off that e-mail to me and my publisher, let me explain. I don't think what I'm saying is that much of a stretch from what many already believe. I am just saying it in a way that you may not have heard before.

Six years ago, I was in my first year as a school principal. I had spent the previous three years as an assistant principal learning the ropes of managing adults and trying to inspire growth and change, but I still had much to learn. As a young (thirty-three year old), first-year principal, I felt I had a lot to prove. I was working in a school that had stagnated in terms of student achievement data. We had amazing teachers doing amazing things, but we were just not seeing the results. I was a believer, and still am, that the greatest way to inspire change is to provide great descriptive feedback. As an administrator, that meant I needed to use the teacher evaluation process as more than a means to label teachers as good or bad (satisfactory or unsatisfactory); I needed to provide a reflective lens in which each teacher could grow and develop.

To this date, the single most effective evaluation I ever conducted was my first. As a new principal, I made a calculated decision to start the evaluation process with what I thought would be an easy path. I wanted to observe the teachers who had the best reputations, those whom everyone believed were doing a great job, and validate everything they were doing well. I wanted to use these teachers as guinea pigs. I thought these teachers would be a piece of cake. Boy was I wrong, but it was in the most amazing way possible.

The first observation I went on was career changing, and as a matter of fact, it was the inspiration for this book. The teacher I observed had her students engaged and interacting. There was student-owned collaboration and student facilitation of classroom management. The teacher's classroom was a well-oiled machine. She was doing so many things the way teacher-prep programs across the country would want every teacher doing them.

As I began wrapping up my forty-minute observation during which I believed I had just witnessed a master teacher, I noticed something near the classroom door that generated a series of questions that changed my perspective of teaching, assessing, and learning forever. When I describe what this was, some of you will think, *Really? That's it? That's not a big deal at all.* But it is often in the seemingly mundane details that we can begin to uncover the largest truths. In two words written on this teacher's monthly calendar, a calendar I didn't even notice until I was walking out of the room, I uncovered a reality that has changed the course of my career.

This teacher was extremely organized. She was the envy of her peers because of her ability to have a lesson plan crafted for every day for an entire month. She had parent phone numbers on a rolodex on her desk and had a reputation for returning all student work within twenty-four hours. Her organization was wonderful; that became the pivot point for all future conversations about effective teaching and learning at that school.

On a bulletin board just inside the door of this teacher's classroom was an assignment calendar that listed upcoming sporting events, band concerts, homework, and field trips. She also was so organized that on this given day she was able to write that the following Friday (I remember this observation was on a Thursday—eight days prior to the day being described) were written two words: "Test Day." She had planned her instruction so far in advance that she knew what her students would be doing eight days later. As a matter of fact, I learned that she actually wrote that date on the calendar the week before. "Test day": two words written on a bulletin board calendar have inspired every presentation I have made since that day.

Seeing those two words sent my mind racing in many directions. I look back on it now and say I had no idea what I was thinking, but I simply knew I wanted to know more. Taking a page out of my law professor's playbook, I asked the teacher a bunch of questions during our follow-up conversation after first complimenting her for her attention to detail and organization. I asked this great teacher, "How do you know your students will be ready for a test next week?" This was an innocent question intending no judgment whatsoever, but I'm sure it came across more like asking your grandfather at Thanksgiving dinner, "So tell me, why are you a Democrat?"

After hearing the teacher's explanation about all the instruction she would be providing to her students each of the next seven days and all the informal assessments she would be administering as a part of each day's lesson plan, I asked, "If you know what the kids will know, why do you need to test them?" She looked puzzled. "If you don't know your students will be ready, why give them a test?" I was on a roll. I didn't realize it at the time, but I had just stumbled on the test giver's Catch 22—a series of questions whose answers only complicate the prior responses. Do you give a test only when you know the students already know it all, or do you give a test when you don't know what the students know? If your students already have proven to you what they know, are you giving a test just because you feel you're supposed to? Are tests given to prove something that you think you already know or to confirm a hunch? In the real world, the answer is that we give tests only when other evidence has already confirmed something.

I have four kids. I know a thing or two about pregnancy tests. I know that most women do not wake up every Friday, pull test kits out of their medicine cabinets, and pee on sticks just to see if they're pregnant. I apologize for the crudeness of this example, but few women take a pregnancy test unless they have some other cues prompting them to. More than likely, a woman will take a pregnancy test only if she already feels she knows the result; the test provides confirmation one way or the other.

We have too many teachers who simply open their file cabinets on Friday and tell their students to take a test with no indicators letting the teachers know it's the appropriate time and with no plan for what to do once they get the results. My wife told me that each time she took a pregnancy test, she spent the three to five minutes waiting for the results thinking of how she would tell me another child was on the way, coming up with baby names, and trying to figure out if she'd be disappointed or relieved with the results either way. For her, the tests were a confirmation of a hunch predicated by other evidence that led to future action.

In our classrooms, we need to stop giving tests and as a result of them label our students as "got it" or "failing", "smart" or "delayed, and start using tests to see how our students are learning and progressing and to help determine what we as teachers can do about it. We need to stop trying to determine whether our students have memorized every word we have said or every word they have read and start focusing on where our students are in becoming learners.

Testing learning is not the same as testing for pregnancy, in which we can simply label the results positive or negative; testing learning is more like measuring the growth of a child with an ultrasound and comparing that to an anticipated due date. As teachers, we help students conceive an initial thought, and our job then has to be to provide frequent and regular well visits to ensure growth and vitality. If we see areas of concern, we intervene and remediate. This is a different way of thinking for many, but so important.

We need to stop worrying about knowledge and start worrying about learning. If we value it, we test it. If our mission statements say we are to create lifelong learners, we need to start measuring our ability to do that and stop measuring whether our students have memorized a bunch of text. Memorizing a spelling word does not create a person with an affinity for learning. Memorizing the dates of Civil War battles does not help students learn how to avoid similar conflicts in the future. We must begin to see all assessments as formative and must be willing to see all learning as a process rather than a yes-or-no proposition. Learning is not as simple as "Got it" or "Nope." All learning builds upon prior foundations and requires new understanding in order to progress. The job of a second-grade teacher is not only to provide seven-year-olds with a prescribed set of learning but also to build a foundation for the learning that will occur in third grade.

As parents, our job is not to create perfect kids but to provide the building blocks for future successful adults. Teachers at every level must first embrace the process of learning and cast off the illusion that our job is to get children to simply memorize facts.

Chapter 10

Don't Label Your Box

At my school, we did an activity that required each staff member to bring in a picture of himself or herself from middle school to display along with the following message: "It's not about who you were, it's who you are that determines who you will be." This activity helped us show our students who we were as children and give them hope for their future. Beyond that, it allowed each of us a chance to take a trip down memory lane by flipping through old photo albums. While I was flipping through one of mine, I stumbled upon a picture I had long ago forgotten. It was an image of me at age twelve sitting in a box.

I grew up as a navy brat. Having a father who served in the military meant that my family relocated frequently. I attended sixteen schools growing up. While we were relocating, so were all our household goods. I spent a great deal of my childhood packing and unpacking. The image in that photo was of me soon after having made one of our many moves. My family had just moved into a new house, and all my toys and clothes had just been delivered. I'd been asked to spend a month surviving with only the items that could fit into one suitcase. On the day the picture was taken, all my other personal possessions had arrived—toys, clothes, sports equipment, everything.

When my parents took the picture with what I assume was a recently unpacked camera, they figured I would be playing with my newfound toys, but they saw my toys out of the box and me sitting in it wearing sunglasses and a backward hat; I'd turned that packing box into a fighter jet, and I was the pilot.

What the picture did not show was that the next day, that box was a racecar, and the next day, it was King Tut's tomb. That box sparked hours of creative fun. Was that what the manufacturer of that box intended? No way. It was designed to hold personal items for easy shipping. My parents had even labeled it Dave's Toys. But with my imagination, I turned it into so much more.

What does that have to do with teaching and learning? It's a metaphor for what is and isn't working in our schools today. Teachers today are constantly looking for the silver bullet to student engagement, student learning, student inquiry, student assessment, etc. We read articles, explore Twitter, and attend conferences hoping to hear about the trick necessary to increase our bottom line—student achievement. Unfortunately, what we often do as a result of all this learning is place ourselves in a box, slap a label on it, and lose our creativity. We think one initiative, one tool, one properly packaged and labeled program will be the answer. We try to find a script to follow; we forget we have kids to reach, and we become frustrated when we don't get the intended results.

A prime example is the work being done with assessment today. For the past ten years, the terms *formative* and *summative* assessments have been used by countless so-called experts to describe how we need to evaluate student learning. Teachers often learn about these two formats and try to craft two types of assessments to fit their varied needs. We are told that teachers must create a formative assessment if they want to evaluate teacher effectiveness. We are told that teachers must create summative assessments if they want to evaluate student learning. We place these assessments in two boxes, label them, and use them only for our preplanned purposes.

Don't get me wrong here; using formative and summative assessments are crucial components of high-quality teaching. We've spent the last four years at my school talking about little else, but we lose sight of the fact that the best assessments serve both purposes, not one exclusively. Placing a label on an assessment prior to using the assessment is unnecessarily restricting. Teachers should be able to give an assessment and use it formatively and summatively. The label on the assessment should not be applied until it has been used. Placing it on prematurely puts us in a box with a big label.

If we label it summative and don't get results indicating student learning, does this mean a teacher should not adjust his or her instruction? If we label it formative but every kid shows mastery, are we not supposed to claim this as evidence of proficiency? A great assessment allows us to use it formatively to evaluate our own instruction *and* summatively by assessing student understanding. It is how the task is used, not how it is designed, that yields results.

Assessment is critical. Teachers must be diligent when it comes to determining the validity and reliability of an assessment, but that doesn't mean they must limit themselves to labels. When working on classroom instruction, teachers must not fool themselves that there is only one way for children to learn. There are countless ways for students to learn just as there are countless ways for students to show what they have learned. We need to avoid putting our students in boxes that are already labeled. We need to avoid telling students there is only one way to do anything. We need to know how the story of our classroom will unfold, but we may not necessarily know the themes that will emerge.

Great authors understand this. They don't title their books before they write them; they wait until they've developed an entire plot and then look for a way to synthesize the message. Singers do not determine which songs will be singles or the titles of their albums until the entire record has been crafted. Teachers need to learn to take our labels off and just go.

I think about my oldest son, who likes to play with Legos. He has countless sets and bricks of every shape and color. His sets come in boxes with directions. He used to follow the directions, assemble the pieces just right, and then … nothing. Once he had followed the manufacturer's directions, he saw his job as done. He was not asked to be creative, inventive, or investigative. We now buy his Legos, toss the directions in the garbage, throw the pieces into a bin with the rest of them, and say, "Have fun!" It's up to him to learn, create, and think outside the box.

The kids we're teaching today will be asked to demonstrate that they understand the world in a way that is much different from what ours was back when. Sure, they will need to follow directions, but more than that, they will be asked to write directions; they'll be asked to identify problems and create solutions. They'll be asked to serve as engineers in some capacity. They will be asked to design solutions, experiment, troubleshoot, and fail repeatedly.

As teachers, we must not put ourselves or our students in labeled boxes. Of course, we need to stay organized, but the only time a box needs a label is when items are being moved from one place to another. Once it's arrived, we can scrub the labels off and let the creativity begin.

Don't force your students to learn the way you learn; let them learn how to learn. Don't force them to be assessed using one template; let them demonstrate understanding by being creative. Help them identify the problems, but let them generate the solutions. Don't stick to the script when an ad lib is necessary. Don't tell your students to climb out of the box because it was designed for something else. If your students climb in, help them create something that has value.

I'm lucky that that day thirty-some years ago, my parents let my toys sit on the bedroom floor and captured a picture of me playing in an empty box that allowed my creative energies to be utilized. I'd repurposed a box that had been designed for one purpose, and that idea has stuck with me since. Once the label Dave's Toys was removed, that box became so many other things; it's now a great memory that has changed the way I parent, teach, and lead.

How can you give your students access to an empty, unlabeled box?

Chapter 11

Keeping Learning on Par

I love to play golf even though I'm not very good at it. I know I'm not very good because someone a long time ago created a scoring system that reminds me that my scores are well above average, and in golf, being above average is not a good thing. The goal is to get my ball into the hole in as few strokes as possible. Doing so at an average level would make me on par with others. I am well over par. Despite this, I can have a great time playing eighteen holes. I end up getting my ball into the cup every time, but I know I'm still not very good based on the number of strokes it takes me to do that.

One of the great things about golf is that excellence is defined the same way for everyone because everyone faces the same obstacles and same opportunities. The water hazards, sand traps, and the wide fairways on every course I've played were designed and constructed years before I picked up a club. It's each golfer vs. the course. The course's goal is not to beat me; my goal is to beat the course.

Course designers come up with eighteen holes that a par golfer can play in seventy or seventy-two shots. On any given hole, par will be between three and five shots depending on the challenge and length. Golf courses often supply golfers with scorecards that depict each hole and even suggested shots for maneuvering from the first shot at the tee box to the hole on the green to help them reach par on that hole. Often, the course itself offers support by providing information along the way by indicating when a golfer is within 150 yards of the green or "almost there."

Golfers are provided a scorecard before beginning their rounds on which they self-monitor and chart their progress. When players keep score, they typically write a few things on their cards. They write the number of shots it took to sink their ball into the hole, and they may include some comments regarding whether they were over or under par, how many putts they hit, and so on, but not much more. They don't document every swing, whether they hit a three wood or a driver, whether they used a nine iron or wedge, whether the wind was blowing or the sun was shining. They identify their success in relation to the expected standard of par and move on.

Each time they play, they aim to improve their score by getting closer to par or perhaps if they are advanced even getting under par, the norm. Most recreational golfers don't play with a course official watching their every swing and verifying the accuracy of their scorecards at the end of the round. It is up to the golfers to be honest.

If my ball ever gets buried under an inch of grass, nobody will remove me from the course and label me a failure if I bend down and remove my ball from the hazard to make my next shot easier. But I'll be cheating myself; the accuracy of my score and its validity by which it is compared to others will have been tainted.

Grading and scoring in an American public-school system shouldn't be much different. Each state has identified its standards and expectations for each child. These aren't secrets. It's the job of the teacher to provide the map and strategy for successfully maneuvering from standard to standard. There should be no surprises or secrets. It's not a race to simply cover the curriculum just as it's not a race to just get eighteen holes behind us. It should be the goal to make every lesson count just as every shot counts. All it takes is one moment with a lapse in focus to send us wandering through the wilderness, the rough.

Documenting student success should also not be done arbitrarily. The standards are defined. Students should be told succinctly whether they have failed, met, or surpassed the standard. Are they up to par? If not, let them know how to take a different shot in the future and welcome them back to the course at another time to play the hole again and demonstrate improved performance. If they do, the new score counts. Even die-hard golfers take mulligans every once in a while.

Students must be given the feedback needed to know how to improve. If their shot end them up in a hazard, make them hit from there. It's okay if they struggle or don't hit it the first time. The goal is for them to learn from their mistakes. If we constantly put some students on a miniature golf course where the greatest hazard is a windmill and others are forced to play on a course resembling a Scottish meadow, we're not providing them the feedback necessary to document their progress. It's okay to let some students hit their first shots from a tee box a little closer to the hole and to make others students hit from farther back, but that needs to be reported, and this can be adjusted from hole to hole. The job of a good classroom teacher is to identify each child's strengths and put him or her in a position to capitalize on them for future growth and success.

The bottom line is that student success—obtaining it and documenting it alike—should not be a mystery. Whether your experience with golf is hitting an orange ball across synthetic grass at a carnival or hitting a driver down the fairway at the Masters, we can all learn a lot about how to demonstrate mastery of standards from the great game of golf.

Chapter 12

Student Engagement-From Dating to Commitment

B uzzwords and acronyms abound in education. PBIS, RTI, differentiation, standards, assessment, PLCs—the list goes on. One of the latest buzzwords getting a lot of airtime is *engagement*. Teachers are asked to assess student engagement regularly. Administrators profess a desire to evaluate student engagement. But does anybody actually know what student engagement looks like? What is it really?

I've heard some people describe student engagement as student activity. Others have described it as students displaying happiness for learning. If you were to ask ten teachers to describe what student engagement looks like, you'd most likely get ten different responses. The same is probably true if you were to ask school administrators—those charged with evaluating teachers—whether student engagement is evident in teachers' classrooms.

We need a consistent definition and way of measuring student engagement so consistent feedback can be given and teachers who work to increase student engagement—an agreed-upon best practice—can know what they're working toward.

Think about it this way. If you're married, what did it mean when you got engaged? If you're single, what will it mean to you to get engaged? Is getting engaged the same thing as getting married? Is it the same thing as dating? What does it mean?

I've been married for sixteen years after an engagement of a year and a half. There are three distinct eras I can identify in my relationship with my wife. When we were dating, I did not wake up every morning and ask myself whether I was happy in my relationship and whether I wanted to continue with it. We spent time together, got to know each other, and began to understand each other on a deeper level. Eventually, we reached decision time. Were we at the place where we were willing to make a commitment no longer contingent on our feelings? Were we willing to say we promised to make things work and continue to learn and grow together even if some mornings we woke up and we were not happy or even liking each other?

When we decided this was the type of commitment we were ready for, we got engaged. Our engagement lasted just long enough for us to get all our proverbial ducks in a row. We made sure that we had jobs lined up, that we would have a house to live in, and that the wedding ceremony was all set up. The wedding was a symbolic gesture by which we publicly shared all we had already committed to. Fourteen years into our marriage, we take all we learned previously and all we continue to learn and apply it in new and more meaningful ways.

Dating is about getting to know someone more and more. Engagement is all about making a commitment. A wedding is all about putting that commitment on display. In a classroom, the initial, superficial learning that occurs on a topic is the equivalent of dating. It's a chance to simply explore an unknown topic in limited ways. This introductory learning is a necessary step that must occur before greater commitment can occur. It's not fair to assume that an engagement should occur before dating has occurred. In a classroom, students may not be engaged unless they have had an introduction to learning. At some point though, students must make a commitment—they must become engaged, that is, show a willingness to learn no matter what gets in the way.

Students should show a willingness to apply the knowledge they learned while dating and a commitment to grow. They should do this in spite of how they feel. They should do this in spite of the activity. They show this by getting all their ducks in a row before the big day, the point of no return.

To throw more academic jargon into this, there will be a lot of formative assessment taking place if students are truly engaged. During an engagement, a couple has the chance to learn how to overcome obstacles, how to endure, and how to plan for success. When they marry, they enter a legally binding contract that says they know how to make it work.

In the classroom, this may be the moment when a summative assessment is given. This may be a public performance, a paper-and-pencil test or any other assessment trick used by a teacher, to publicly share what they've learned as a result of their engagement.

So what is the best way to assess whether students are engaged? It goes way beyond looking for smiles or movement. It goes beyond looking at the activities or assignments. True engagement is a commitment to learning. If students are engaged, they will be reluctant to leave the classroom. They won't be absent. They'll talk about the subject matter in the hallways and at home. The best way to determine whether students are engaged is to test their commitment to learn.

Life is full of tests. In America, we give a lot of attention to the jobs of doctors and lawyers. We encourage children to pursue these career paths believing them to be truly professional roles that reap big paychecks and society's respect. Doctors and lawyers are among our most educated citizens, and as such, we expect them to give evidence of a high level of expertise. We go into our doctors' offices expecting more than just lectures on healthy living. We expect to have someone trained to assess our health and provide a patient-centric plan for improvement. We don't want lawyers who will simply take any case and tie up the legal system with time-wasting efforts; we want attorneys capable of collecting evidence, drawing rational and logical cases, and providing compelling visions of what the evidence says. Compare our expectations of those two professions to what most of society expects of teachers. What I have seen across the country is that most teachers are not given the training in how to assess students, how to collect evidence, how to provide feedback on the evidence, or how to provide patient centric plans. Teachers are asked to help develop our future professionals and yet have often not been given the proper training to make professional decisions themselves.

Districts spend thousands providing teachers with binders, posters, textbooks, and training on how to implement the latest silver-bullet plan. Teachers are not given the guidance afforded to other professionals to work effectively and yet we wonder why our students are not progressing. If the vast majority of a doctor's patients were dying, we would expect an audit not just of his treatment plans but also of his plans for diagnosis. Why was he not catching the ailments of his patients sooner thus preventing further complications? We know that proper diagnosis leads to proper treatment. We wouldn't expect the doctor to just be given more posters to line his office walls or more informational pamphlets for the patients to read in the lobby.

For some reason though, this is exactly what we have done in America's schools. I know this because I have a side job as an adjunct professor for a small college in its education department teaching courses on the use of assessment to drive instruction. My courses are all in the graduate program of the college; most of my students are already teachers. The courses are reserved for those pursuing an advanced degree or administrative credentials. Those on the front lines of educating our nation's youth, our current classroom teachers, are often given training from their undergraduate programs in their major discipline subject area. They may receive a little instruction on lesson planning and pedagogical theory, but they are left at a disadvantage when trying to understand how to gauge and measure student understanding of what they teach and how to use that information to plan their instruction. This guidance is often reserved only for those pursuing advanced degrees or who decide on their own to pick up a book like this one.

Teachers must understand what standard measurements are, how to assess their students, and how to create student-centric plans. Each of these components is essential. We cannot look at any of these components as independent silos. As teachers, we must gain better understanding so we can eventually begin to make informed, evaluative judgments and the creative, dynamic lessons our students deserve.

Teachers are forced to make decisions of instructional bias daily; they are asked to establish priorities and determine the importance of concepts based on their subjective lens or objective data analysis. Just this morning, I ran just three miles before work because I wanted a little extra sleep; I made a decision of value. I valued a little extra sleep. I valued a run over an extra cup of coffee. I valued punctuality over an extra mile on the streets in my jogging shoes.

In your classroom, you make selective decisions daily. What will you place on your bulletin board? Which students will you allow to sit next to each other? What Christmas cookies brought to you by your students will you actually eat and which will you throw into the trash? We have heard before that teaching is an art and a science. Being selective and making wise instructional decisions is the art of teaching. What separates a good artist from a hack is simply decision making. A photographer decides which negative to develop and which to discard. A potter decides which pot to glaze and which to reshape. A painter decides which colors to combine and which to avoid. Effective teachers make similar artistic decisions. They embrace the science of teaching allowing them to quantify data, analyze standards, and evaluate curricula, but they are artists because they can take scientific analysis and make decisions that allow them to change the destinies of their students in ways nobody else can.

In the day and age we live and work, one that elevates the importance of standards and focused learning, we must remember that artists are seen as great only when they are original and difficult to replicate. Artists understand essential standards of color, shape, size, contrast, and texture, yet taking accepted standards and creating something original is what leads to endurance and legacies. Teachers must be willing to take risks and think outside of their proverbial boxes to reach kids as only they can. Teachers teach. Everything else—curricula, texts, assessments, supplies—is simply a tool, not a mandate or requirement for student success. But I'm getting ahead of myself. Just as a great artist can make decisions on quality based only on foundational knowledge of color, texture, shape, and dimension, teachers must first embrace the science of standards and quantifiable evidence before building on this foundation to make solid subjective interpretations.

Teachers are expected to help students gain understanding of selected standards. Your state may have adopted the Common Core State Standards, the Next Generation Science Standards, the C3 Social Studies Framework, or some other variation of standards that politicians got hold of and adapted to meet their political agendas. Regardless of which standards you are asked to teach your students, you are confronted with three realities.

1. There are far too many standards for you as a lone teacher with approximately 180 days of school this year to possibly get through.
2. Every teacher in your building, district, state, and municipality interpret these standards differently.

3. You are more than likely being evaluated in part not just on
    your ability to teach the standards but your students' ability
    to prove they have learned those standards.

It's becoming commonplace for teachers to serve on school
data teams to evaluate a state assessment and students' success, or
probably more accurately, the students they taught last year and
their success and struggles so the teachers can determine deficiencies
and come up with focused plans of attack to remedy those issues in
future years.

It is probably also true that at some point in the last three years,
you were told that the format of your state level test was changing.
Maybe the students will now be tested online. Maybe they will be
given an adaptive test that by nature students will be expected to
get 50 percent of questions wrong on. Maybe the subject areas and
grade levels for the assessment have changed. Maybe you teach a
subject area in which there is no state exam and you have been asked
to develop your own assessment criteria.

You as a teacher, with very little formal training on test validity
and reliability, little understanding of standard deviations, T scores,
percentile rankings, evaluator bias, etc., have been asked to look at
a collection of student scores. You are asked to make sense of them
and make instructional decisions of course with the guidance of
administrators who probably had graduate-level courses in all this
and have the three credit hours to prove their expertise.

As a building administrator, I'm not knocking this process.
I have had similar committees at work in every building I have
worked in. What I am knocking is the belief that these teams have
any lasting value to a teacher's instructional decision making. I am
yet to meet teachers who go home at the end of a day during which
they broke up fights in the cafeteria, had fifteen parent e-mails to
respond to, collected a hundred homework assignments to grade, and
attended a grade-level team meeting during their only forty-minute

break of the day, and on the drive home think, "Wow! Today was a good day. I determined that the median for my state achievement test scores increased by two points."

As teachers, we see the whole picture but live the day to day. We need to evaluate today and determine how it will affect our tomorrow. Teachers should be involved in the process of generating school improvement plans and looking at school-wide data, but this is not what drives the day to day. The best teachers look at individual students, their competence, and their confidence. They look at kids and measure their affect as well as their assessment effect.

I am a firm believer that we should be teaching to the test but not teaching how to test. I have had parents tell me, "My child is not a good test taker." I have looked at teacher gradebooks and have seen some teachers who weight their grades so that tests have a larger impact on total success, or at least as measured by a grade, than do homework and classwork. I have seen some students who never complete daily work but get A's on every test or quiz. I have seen some teachers who never give paper-and-pencil exams but instead give projects and presentations every few weeks.

As teachers, we look at our systems and try to manipulate them to serve our purposes. We value certain tasks and behaviors over others and allow our biases to affect how we assess and provide feedback to our students. When I say I think we should teach to a test, I mean to begin with the end in mind. Tests often provoke a mental image of a quiet classroom with students filling in ovals with their pencils while the teacher sits at a desk. This teacher is just waiting for a child to sneeze so she can rush over and rip up the child's work for obviously using a creative new code to cheat with a friend on the other side of the room.

In the real world in which we all live outside of the sterile confines of a classroom, a test has a much broader definition. I am tested daily by my four children. They may beg for me to respond in an appropriate way to meet their needs. Often driving home, I am confronted with a reckless driver who may cut me off and thus test my driving skills and patience. Life tests me daily, and very rarely am I given a paper and pencil with which to prove my proficiency.

As educators, we are tasked with preparing our students to be successful in the real world, so we need to test them as the real world does. We need to find authentic and meaningful ways to assess their skills, abilities, and attitudes. We need to look at these tests and make informed, artistic decisions that allow us to remediate and advance learning, not just label a child as a success or a failure because of a singular moment in time in which he or she was given a two-sided worksheet on which to regurgitate a bunch of information presented the previous week.

As educators, we must understand what our tests will look like before we begin our instruction and then do all we can to make sure our instruction is helping prepare our students for those tests that may come in a variety of formats, at a variety of times, and in a variety of circumstances.

As a father, I know life is hard and filled with obstacles. I know my children will be asked to display patience and perseverance. I know they will be asked to be honest and trustworthy. I may not be able to predict when or how they will be asked to demonstrate these things, but I know the tests will be coming.

As they grow up, I am ever on the lookout for them to demonstrate how much of these attributes they have absorbed and retained so I can provide reteaching or greater understanding. As a classroom teacher, I must do the same. I must first come to an understanding of what the test is, or at least what will be tested, and make constant adjustments to my instruction to ensure that my students will be ready when tested. I won't focus all my attention on a specific format of a test but instead be sure that my students have a thorough understanding of the content so that no matter the format, they will be able to show success.

My kids are learning they should show respect to me as their dad not just when they're requesting a new toy. They're learning what respect looks and sounds like to all people at all times so that no matter who is testing them or how they are being tested, they will demonstrate an understanding, and if not, as their dad, I can step in and do some reteaching.

We need to move beyond the days of asking students to study on a Thursday for an exam on Friday but forget everything by Monday. We need to ask ourselves, if this is not important enough for a child to remember beyond my classroom, should I spend time teaching it? If the only guidance I can give a student to learn more is to study more, am I really needed?

As a teacher, you must get comfortable thinking of yourself as the most important item needed in your students' academic life. You are the one who not only determines how items will be taught but also what will be taught.

You have tremendous control over each child's destiny. Research has proven time and again that far beyond curricula, pedagogical tricks, and scheduling frameworks, the greatest factor in determining a child's academic success or failure is the quality of his or her teacher. That is a huge responsibility. As a teacher, you can run away from that responsibility and leave it to textbook manufacturers and career politicians, or you can embrace it and use your knowledge to change the future. You must be willing to move beyond simply reading the standards and looking at quantitative data analysis and the accompanying pacing guide to embrace the art of teaching. Just as learning requires more than just decoding text on a written page, teaching requires far more than facilitating students to complete tasks. Teaching requires the ability to allow students to learn and an understanding that every child will learn differently.

That sounds great, but do teachers really have the power to decide what to teach their students? After all, who are you to decide what the most important thing is for a child to learn and how they are to learn it? You are the teacher; that's who. Now don't get me wrong. I'm not asking anyone to work outside the system currently in place. I am not asking for mutiny and anarchy while every teacher subjectively decides what the most important concepts and subjects are while tossing the rest to the side. That is what we have had for the last fifty years when every elementary teacher taught dinosaurs and every secondary English teacher taught the parts of speech. Teachers cannot just subjectively decide what is interesting or important. I am not asking you to disregard the system but to study the system in place, determine which fights are essential, and work within the current system to change it.

In my current district, for example, fourth-grade teachers are presented with seventy-seven English language arts standards for their students. More than simply learning the standards, students are expected to be able to demonstrate mastery of them by the end of the year. If it were simply about teaching them, a teacher could take one day out of the year, stand in front of her students, and read the curriculum framework aloud. Reading the seventy-seven standards word for word could probably be accomplished in one ninety-minute assembly or two forty-five-minute class periods. Even those teachers who believe their job is to stand behind a podium in the front of the classroom and lecture for a full class period seemingly never even pausing for air would be remiss if they thought simply reading a list of standards would allow their students to gain mastery of any of them. Most teachers understand that teaching goes beyond just speaking. Just as leading requires followers, teaching requires learners. If students are not learning what is being presented to them, no teaching is taking place.

Knowing that a teacher will not be able to simply stand in front of her students and read the standards, how will she be able to ensure all her students have mastered all the standards before she sends them off to the next grade? She could take the 180 days in the school year and divide the seventy-seven standards evenly and every 2.337 days introduce a new standard to the students. She could then wait until the state-mandated spring assessment is given, place her students in front of the test, and have full confidence they will show mastery of every standard.

In Florida, where I currently work full-time, as in the majority of states today, teachers have their professional evaluations tied to their student performance on these end-of-year tests. As a result, teachers would be foolish not to do all they could to help their students show success if even for simple career advancement. Even if a teacher is not altruistic enough to believe his job can change a child's life, he should understand that his own job appraisal may depend on his ability to get students to show success on the end of course test. So why does this strategy of quickly covering every standard in a predetermined time frame advocated by anyone other than textbook companies?

A quick review of current research on the most effective instructional practices argues for the opposite. If you don't believe me, take another break from reading this and do a quick Google search for "teaching effect size." From this quick search, you will find study after study that shows the most successful approaches are those that allow for greater student voice and control; translated, that means less teacher control.

As teachers who are concerned about our evaluations who also have the moral imperative to help every child grow in a meaningful way, why are we content to let textbook publishers, our greatest competition in the field of student learning, determine how best to educate our kids? We must take a stand for what we know is best for our kids. Teachers teach. Students learn.

In our schools, we have let our fiscal resources rather than our human resources determine our future. Our books, supplies, and technologies are all resources to help teachers, not to control or constrain them. These are all clothes in our proverbial closet to help us dress up our teaching. If something doesn't fit you, it doesn't mean it won't fit someone else; it means you need to try on something different—maybe your comfy jeans and favorite T-shirt. Sometimes, we need to wake up early and iron out what we are putting on. Sometimes, we need to look in a mirror and reflect on how we are presenting ourselves. One size does not fit all; we need to move beyond believing anything other than that.

Teaching is hard work, but it is also extremely rewarding if done right. We need to realize that fashion comes and goes and that what fit last year may not fit this year, but we won't know until we try it on. We must get accustomed to identifying what we need to wear, how to check the proverbial weather forecast and dress code, and how to measure for a best fit. We can tell teachers every day to reflect and be student centered, to differentiate their instruction and plan with the end in mind, but unless we teach teachers how to do that, we may still be wearing the clothes and teaching the lessons that worked for us twenty years ago. For the record, bell-bottoms, like worksheets for homework, should never come back in style.

Teachers have to embrace their power and responsibility along with the obligation of intentional planning. Teachers cannot simply say something to kids one time or in this case repeat a standard repeatedly for 2.337 days and expect every child to learn it. That is not how learning happens.

Teachers often resort to one of two approaches. They either shrug off the responsibility of making instructional decisions because they believe that's above their pay grade and beyond their control and just follow a textbook page for page, limiting the positive impact a great teacher could have on a child's success. Or they choose standards to teach their students based on their own personal interests or the exciting projects they can get the kids involved in.

As a classroom teacher, I was guilty of both approaches. Some days (months) I was just too tired to make lesson plans and would ask my students to read a textbook and answer the questions at the end of every section just so I could have grades to enter into the grade book. But other times, I'd come up with fun projects (today, that would involve a Pinterest or Twitter search), go backward, and identify what standards I could possibly connect to the cool poster project I discovered the night before.

It was a rare day that I would sit down, analyze the standards predetermined for my grade and subject area, evaluate their relevance and impact, rank order them, and then determine which one to teach tomorrow and how to do so for the greatest impact. Actually, that was something I didn't do until my last couple of years in the classroom, but it was exactly what I should have been doing all along if only I had known better, if only I had been taught to embrace the power I truly had in a classroom, the power to change destinies.

Chapter 13

Bold Humility: The Best Teachers Are Oxymorons

We teachers sometimes struggle with embracing our power. We're used to having classrooms of kids look up at us from their desks presuming that we are the smartest ones in the rooms, yet for some reason, we often struggle to embrace the influence we have. We are such rule followers that often times embracing our ability to think for ourselves is a real struggle. As a building leader, I spend the bulk of my time trying to create a sense of bold humility in teachers. Bold humility is the unique character trait that separates the great from the good. It is that "it" factor that we often talk about when we find teachers who have mastered their craft. They are bold enough to say they are the most important factor in changing a kid's life yet humble enough to realize their opinions may not always be right. They have confidence in their influence but humility in their actions.

In my schools, these teachers are embraced as change agents for the schools and given individualized coaching in how to make decisions about instructional bias. I foster and encourage their abilities to make decisions. I want them to embrace their power so they can harness it for good.

Teachers are superheroes who must understand their influence so they can maximize it for the good of kids. A superpower not properly harnessed can be a destructive force, a hurricane, a super villain. Power embraced and used for good can change the world for the better. These teachers are afforded the opportunity to use their power to analyze the academic standards assigned to their subject areas and grade levels to make decisions of priority and change kids' lives one lesson at a time.

Soon after my teachers begin to realize their power and influence, they are asked to begin making some critical instructional decisions. Before teachers start deciding how they will teach (the art of teaching), they are asked to examine what to teach (the science of teaching). As was discussed earlier in this book, in my schools, we use the term *power standards* to describe those standards that we believe are the most essential for student success. In other schools, I have heard them referred to as essential learnings, priority standards, or even must-knows. These are the standards the teachers have determined to be the most critical of all standards.

Knowing for example that there is not enough time in a school year to teach each of the seventy-seven ELA standards identified to be taught in a fourth-grade classroom to the depth required for every student to gain mastery of them, the power standards are the standards that classroom teachers determine to be the most powerful. In some districts, these standards are chosen by looking at state assessments and picking the standards that are tied to the most questions on the standardized exam. In some districts, these standards are chosen by asking teachers which standards they enjoy teaching the most. In my buildings, we ask which standards teachers are willing to stake their careers on. We aren't looking to add to our list of available standards; instead we look at those given to us and determine which have the most value. Which standards do we want our students to understand beyond any single test? Which allow students to apply their foundational knowledge across disciplines? Which standards are deep and meaningful?

To make these decisions, educators first need to gain a greater understanding of what the standards actually mean. Teachers can't just read through the complex verbiage of the standards and make a gut-level decision. Standards not only show what content needs to be introduced but also to what depth that should happen. As they are written now, standards go beyond stating the content to be addressed; now, they commonly include what the students will be expected to do with the content. The standards show the knowledge students must be able to recall and what they should be able to do with it. Should they understand, apply, analyze, synthesize, evaluate, or create?

Using the framework of Bloom's Taxonomy, an educator can do a quick analysis of the standards and determine which carry the obligation of high-order thinking. Which standards ask students to do more than memorize facts? Memorizing facts is something a student can do independently and probably does not require the help of a teacher. Better yet, students can simply look up the facts when they need them. Gaining basic knowledge of a concept can be accomplished by reading a book or completing a worksheet. Standards that require a highly competent, life-changing, inspiring teacher are those that require greater depth and in turn are those that are the most essential for the classroom teacher to address.

Teachers can then classify their seventy-plus standards into categories based on their complexity. This may only mean that teachers are able to move standards into two categories—high-order and low-order—but this is a huge head start in determining what standards may be more critical.

Even if the list of essential standards is cut in half by examining only those identified as "high order", teachers may still be overwhelmed. Teaching one standard per week to a mastery level (the average school year is 38 weeks) is not much easier than doing so every 2.3 days (if each of the seventy plus standards were taught in a one hundred-eighty day school year). Somehow, this needs to be reduced even further or teachers will fall into the trap of teaching Monday through Thursday and testing on Friday simply to label success or failure and moving on to new content every Monday. This is exactly what is being done in so many classrooms today, and it is not working.

In my schools, at each grade level, in each subject area, teachers identify their top ten standards. Ten that they will teach to mastery, ten that they are willing to guarantee eighty percent of their kids will be proficient in. In a fourth grade classroom that means teachers are now moving their focus from covering seventy seven standards, to ensuring the learning of at least ten. The shift from covering to learning is paramount to ensuring success. That may seem like a huge reduction in content, but thinking about learning as a process that continues over time, those ten standards multiplied over the years becomes at least ninety standards learned to mastery in each subject area before a student even enters high school. Can you remember ninety things you learned to a mastery level before ninth grade in any subject? You may have been exposed to a lot more than that, but becoming proficient, becoming a master, verified by evidence, is a new ball game, and it can't be done by just picking up a book. It can be done only by applying, analyzing, synthesizing, creating—in short, by doing.

As a teacher, you may be thinking, *I can decide which standards are important and work with my teaching peers to reach consensus. But that doesn't help me actually teach them. Plus, my administration would never allow me to have such autonomy. How can I prove that my students are learning what really matters? My school cares only about big tests at the end of the school year. How can I do this and still work within their system?*

As teachers, we have to prove our significance and impact. We're now expected to prove that learning is happening and that we're having an impact on it. How do we demonstrate that learning is evident, though, if it happens in a variety of ways? How do we do it today?

For years, districts took the easy way out and said they would measure learning by watching and evaluating teachers. Building principals would schedule one or two trips to a teacher's classroom during a school year, study the actions of a classroom teacher and maybe even provide her with some feedback, and give her an evaluation score based on her behaviors. What we found out with the advent of the standards movement, however, was that by only collecting evidence of the teacher, we often made incorrect inferences about student learning. Some came to believe that we needed to have high-impact summative assessments to measure student learning in order to quantify teacher success.

Entrance into higher education is often based on far more than a single test score. Simply getting a good score on an entrance exam like the ACT, SAT, or GRE often only forces an admissions officer to take a deeper look into an applicant's classroom grades, extracurricular activities, and citizenship. There's nothing wrong with using a test as a screener for more information; that's what doctors do. Our troubles begin when we think a singular test provides all the evidence we need. We cannot think that although our students learn material in a number of ways, they should all be prepared to demonstrate it the same way. As is the case with a lawyer proving a case to a jury, it's often an accumulation of evidence that leads to a verdict. There is rarely a singular data point that unilaterally leads to a decision of guilt or innocence in a courtroom. A lawyer collects and presents a variety of evidence to prove a point. There is not one simple test that can be presented to a judge or jury to draw a consistent conclusion.

In our classrooms, we need to remove our own assessment arrogance and get into the evidence-collection business and not the test-grading business. Our job is to assess learning so we can make appropriate instructional decisions. Our job is to help our children learn and grow like never before. We must embrace our power and influence. We must be bold enough to make the decisions necessary and humble enough to seek support.

It is through bold humility that we can make the changes necessary to help our children change their destinies and enter the world they will help create. If we want our learning to endure and last a lifetime we cannot continue to focus our attention on methods and strategies that have never really worked. If we want our kids to learn skills that will last beyond a single test, let's teach them the same way we teach them to ride a bike, after all, once you learn how to ride, you never forget.

About the Author

David M. Schmittou, Ed.D., has spent more than two decades in education as a classroom teacher, at-risk coordinator, gifted student coordinator, assistant principal, principal, coach, and college professor. His insights help professional educators to supercharge their careers while taking student learning to the next level.

Printed in the United States
By Bookmasters